ATLASES OF THE WORLD

ATLAS OF
NORTH
AMERICA

TINA LUNDGREN, MALCOLM PORTER, and KEITH LYE

rosen publishing's
rosen
central

This edition published in 2010 by:

The Rosen Publishing Group, Inc.
29 East 21st Street
New York, NY 10010

Library of Congress Cataloging-in-Publication Data

Lundgren, Tina
Atlas of North America / Tina Lundgren, Malcolm Porter,
   and Keith Lye.
   p. cm. – (Atlases of the world)
Includes index.

   ISBN 978-1-4358-8458-8 (library binding)
   ISBN 978-1-4358-9115-9 (pbk.)
   ISBN 978-1-4358-9121-0 (6-pack)

1. North America–Maps. I. Porter, Malcolm.
   II. Lye, Keith. III. Rosen Central (Firm) IV. Title.

G1105.L8 2010
912.7–dc22

                                        2009582103

Manufactured in China

This edition published under license from
Cherrytree Books.

CPSIA Compliance Information: Batch #EW0102YA: For Further Information
contact Rosen Publishing, New York, New York at 1-800-237-9932

ATLASES OF THE WORLD
ATLAS OF NORTH AMERICA

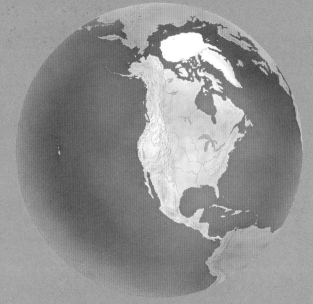

This illustrated atlas combines maps, pictures, flags, globes,
information panels, diagrams and charts to give an overview
of the whole continent and a closer look at each of its countries.

COUNTRY CLOSE-UPS

Each double-page spread has these
features:

Introduction The author introduces the
most important facts about the country
or region.

Globes A globe on which you can see the
country's position in the continent and the
world.

Flags Every country's flag is shown.

Information panels Every country has
an information panel that gives its area,
population and capital, and where possible
its other main towns, languages, religions,
government and currency.

Pictures Important features of each
country are illustrated and captioned to
give a flavor of the country. You can
find out about physical features, famous
people, ordinary people, animals, plants,
places, products, and much more.

Maps Every country is shown on a
clear, accurate map. To get the most from
the maps it helps to know the symbols
that are shown in the key on the
opposite page.

Land You can see by the coloring on
the map where the land is forested,
frozen or desert.

Height Relief hill shading shows where
the mountain ranges are. Individual
mountains are marked by a triangle.

Direction All of the maps are drawn
with north at the top of the page.

Scale All of the maps are drawn to scale
so that you can find the distance
betweeen places in miles or kilometers.

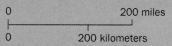

KEY TO MAPS

CANADA	Country name
TEXAS	Province or state name
～～～	Country border
■	More than 1 million people*
●	More than 500,000 people
•	Less than 500,000 people
	Country capital
★	State or province capital
ROCKY MTS	Mountain range
▲ *Mt McKinley* 20,322ft (6,194m)	Mountain with its height
∴ *Tikal*	Archaeological site

Ohio	River
	Canal
	Lake
	Dam
	Island

	Forest
	Crops
	Dry grassland
	Desert
	Tundra
	Polar

*Population figures in all cases are estimates, based on the most recent censuses where available or a variety of other sources.

CONTINENT CLOSE-UPS

People and Beliefs Map of population densities; chart of percentage of population per country; chart of areas of countries; map of religions; chart of main religious groups.

Climate and Vegetation Map of vegetation from polar to desert; map of winter and summer temperatures; map of annual rainfall; diagram of mountain climates.

Ecology and Environment Map of environmental problems and disasters; map of earthquake zones, volcanoes, hurricanes and tornadoes; diagram on greenhouse effect; panel on endangered animals and plants.

Economy Map of agricultural and industrial products; chart of gross domestic products for individual countries; panel on per capita gross domestic products; map of sources of energy.

Politics and History Map of political systems; panel of great events; timeline of important dates; panel showing Viking longboat and Voyager space probe; map of location of major events in North American history.

CONTENTS

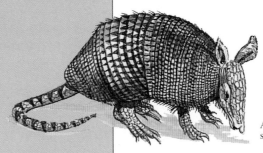

Armadillo
see page 18

NORTH AMERICA

North America is the third largest continent after Asia and Africa. The two biggest countries, Canada and the United States, are among the world's richest. These two high-income countries have many high-tech industries and most people enjoy comfortable lives. Mexico and the countries of Central America and the Caribbean are low- or middle-income countries. Many of their people are poor.

The climate of North America varies greatly from north to south. A huge ice sheet covers most of Greenland in the northeast, with smaller ice caps in northern Canada. The southern parts of North America lie in the hot and humid tropics.

ALASKA
(US)

PACIFIC
OCEAN

Whales swim off the west coast of North America and people enjoy watching them. Many North Americans believe that the development of the land and sea should be controlled so that wildlife and natural wonders can be conserved.

Golden Gate Bridge in San Francisco, California, is one of North America's most famous landmarks. San Francisco was rebuilt after a great earthquake in 1906. Earthquakes and volcanic eruptions occur in western North America and in the Caribbean.

Market days, where farmers sell their produce and buy goods for their families, are important events in Central America. Farming employs more than 30 percent of the people of tropical North America. Many farmers are poor and struggle to survive.

Combine harvesters are used on the huge grain farms of Canada and the United States. Farming is highly mechanized here and employs only two percent of the people. The farms are, however, much more productive than those in the countries to the south.

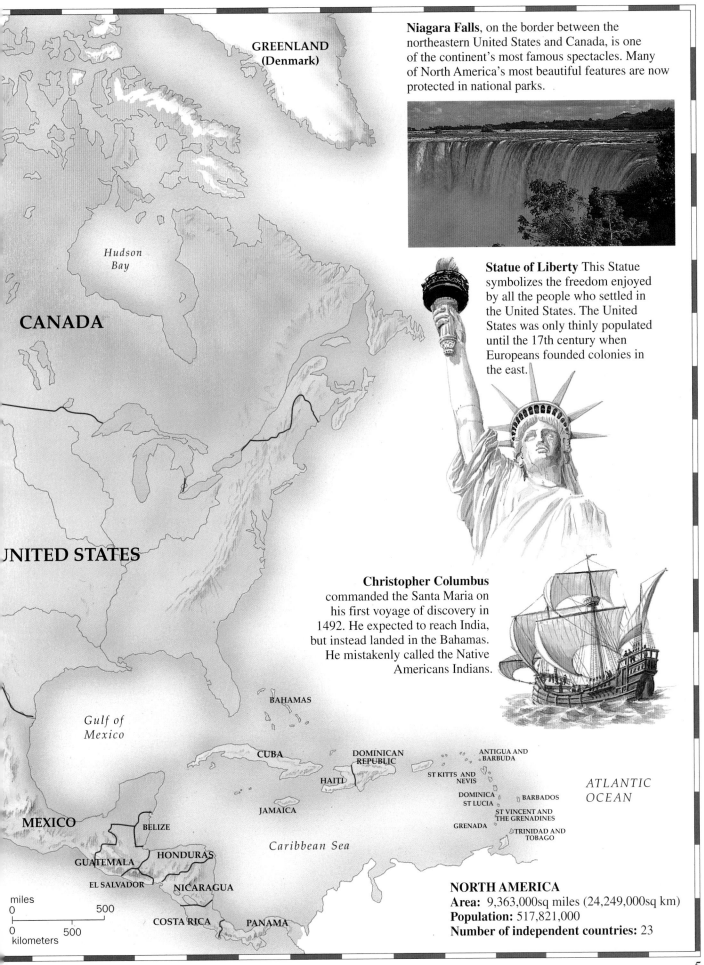

GREENLAND
(Denmark)

Niagara Falls, on the border between the northeastern United States and Canada, is one of the continent's most famous spectacles. Many of North America's most beautiful features are now protected in national parks.

Hudson Bay

CANADA

Statue of Liberty This Statue symbolizes the freedom enjoyed by all the people who settled in the United States. The United States was only thinly populated until the 17th century when Europeans founded colonies in the east.

UNITED STATES

Christopher Columbus commanded the Santa Maria on his first voyage of discovery in 1492. He expected to reach India, but instead landed in the Bahamas. He mistakenly called the Native Americans Indians.

BAHAMAS

Gulf of Mexico

CUBA
DOMINICAN REPUBLIC
ANTIGUA AND BARBUDA
ST KITTS AND NEVIS
HAITI
DOMINICA
ST LUCIA
BARBADOS
ST VINCENT AND THE GRENADINES
JAMAICA
GRENADA
TRINIDAD AND TOBAGO

ATLANTIC OCEAN

MEXICO
BELIZE
Caribbean Sea
GUATEMALA
HONDURAS
EL SALVADOR
NICARAGUA

miles
0   500

0   500
kilometers

COSTA RICA   PANAMA

NORTH AMERICA
Area: 9,363,000sq miles (24,249,000sq km)
Population: 517,821,000
Number of independent countries: 23

CANADA AND GREENLAND

Canada is the world's second largest country. Only Russia is bigger. Much of Canada has long, bitterly cold winters and most Canadians live within 200 miles (320km) of the southern border with the United States. The first people to live in Canada were Native Americans. But most Canadians today are descendants of French and Britishsettlers.

Greenland is the world's largest island. It is a self-governing part of Denmark.

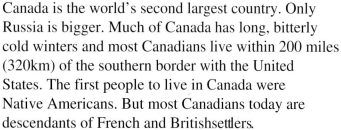

CANADA

Area: 3,851,809sq miles (9,976,139sq km)
Highest point: Mount Logan, 19,849ft (6,050m)
Population: 33,099,000
Capital: Ottawa (pop 1,093,000)
Largest cities: Toronto (4,600,000)
Montreal (3,400,000)
Vancouver (2,000,000)
Official languages: English, French
Religions: Christianity (Roman Catholic 43%, Protestant 23%, Eastern Orthodox 2%), Islam 2%
Government: Federal constitutional monarchy
Currency: Canadian dollar

GREENLAND
Area: 840,000sq miles (2,175,600sq km)
Population: 56,000
Capital: Godthaab
Government: Self-governing part of Denmark

ST PIERRE & MIQUELON
Area: 93sq miles (242sq km)
Population: 7,000
Capital: St Pierre
Government: French territory

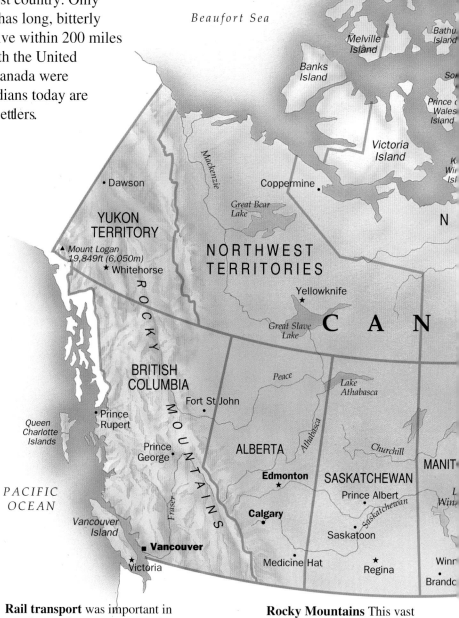

Rail transport was important in opening up the vast country of Canada. The two major companies are the government-owned Canadian National Railway (CN) and the privately owned Canadian Pacific (CP) Railway.

Rocky Mountains This vast range in western Canada has much magnificent scenery. The Pacific Ranges rise to the west of the Rockies. Canada's highest peak, Mount Logan, is in the northwest.

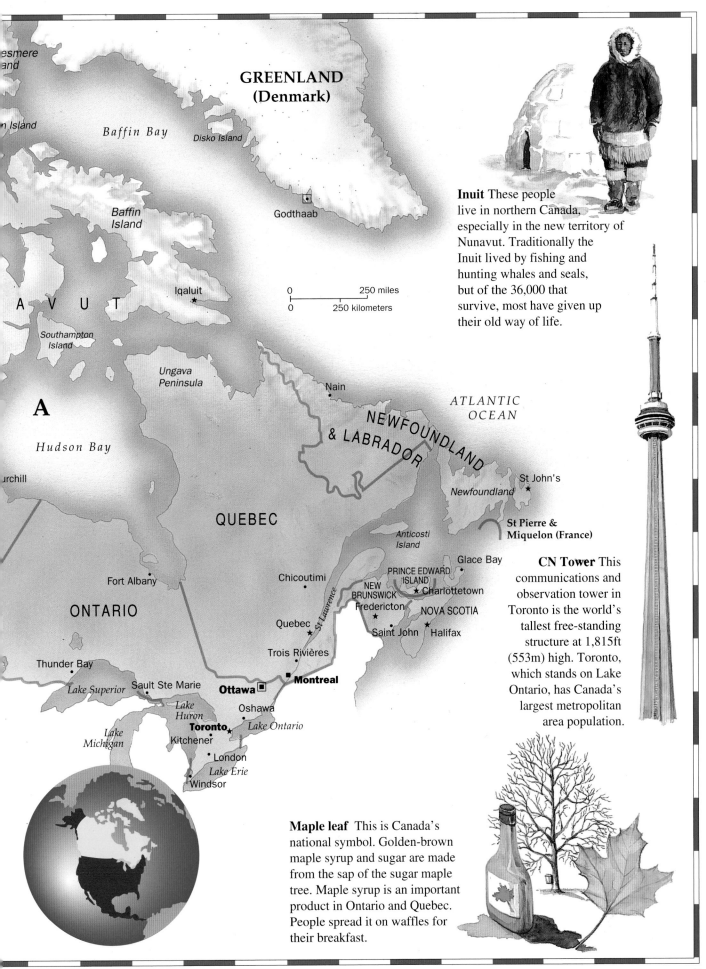

GREENLAND
(Denmark)

Baffin Bay

Disko Island

Godthaab

smere
and

n Island

Baffin Bay

Baffin
Island

A V U T

Iqaluit

0   250 miles
0   250 kilometers

Southampton
Island

A

Ungava
Peninsula

Nain

Hudson Bay

ATLANTIC
OCEAN

NEWFOUNDLAND
& LABRADOR

urchill

St John's

Newfoundland

St Pierre &
Miquelon (France)

QUEBEC

Anticosti
Island

Glace Bay

Fort Albany

Chicoutimi

PRINCE EDWARD
ISLAND

ONTARIO

NEW
BRUNSWICK
Fredericton

Charlottetown

NOVA SCOTIA

Quebec

St Lawrence

Saint John   Halifax

Thunder Bay

Trois Rivières

Lake Superior   Sault Ste Marie

Ottawa

Montreal

Lake
Huron

Oshawa

Lake
Michigan

Toronto

Lake Ontario

Kitchener

London

Lake Erie

Windsor

Inuit These people
live in northern Canada,
especially in the new territory of
Nunavut. Traditionally the
Inuit lived by fishing and
hunting whales and seals,
but of the 36,000 that
survive, most have given up
their old way of life.

CN Tower This
communications and
observation tower in
Toronto is the world's
tallest free-standing
structure at 1,815ft
(553m) high. Toronto,
which stands on Lake
Ontario, has Canada's
largest metropolitan
area population.

Maple leaf This is Canada's
national symbol. Golden-brown
maple syrup and sugar are made
from the sap of the sugar maple
tree. Maple syrup is an important
product in Ontario and Quebec.
People spread it on waffles for
their breakfast.

7

EASTERN CANADA

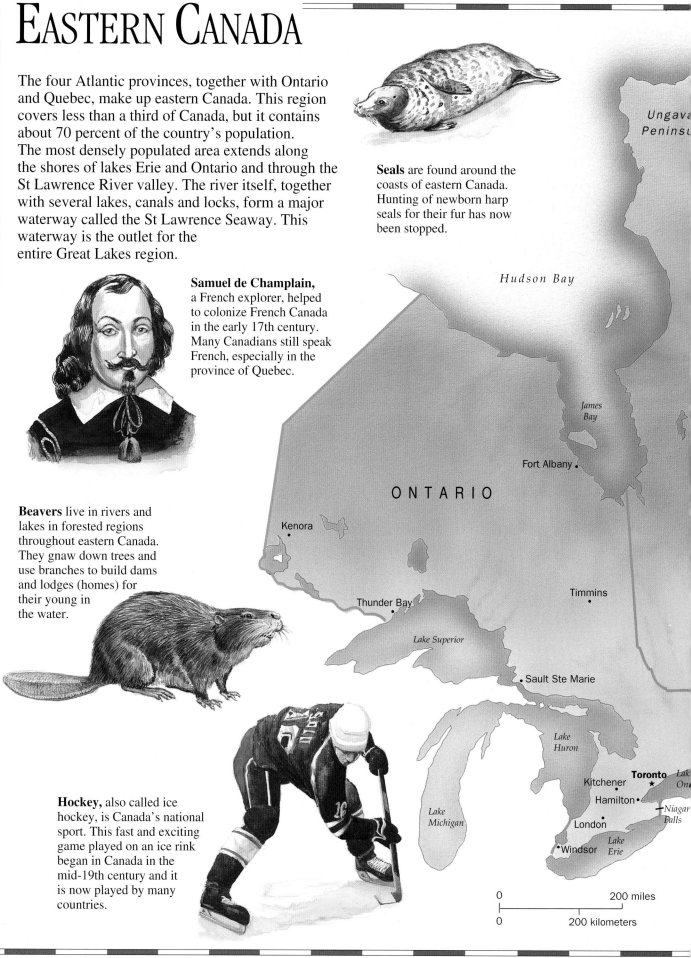

The four Atlantic provinces, together with Ontario and Quebec, make up eastern Canada. This region covers less than a third of Canada, but it contains about 70 percent of the country's population. The most densely populated area extends along the shores of lakes Erie and Ontario and through the St Lawrence River valley. The river itself, together with several lakes, canals and locks, form a major waterway called the St Lawrence Seaway. This waterway is the outlet for the entire Great Lakes region.

Seals are found around the coasts of eastern Canada. Hunting of newborn harp seals for their fur has now been stopped.

Samuel de Champlain, a French explorer, helped to colonize French Canada in the early 17th century. Many Canadians still speak French, especially in the province of Quebec.

Beavers live in rivers and lakes in forested regions throughout eastern Canada. They gnaw down trees and use branches to build dams and lodges (homes) for their young in the water.

Hockey, also called ice hockey, is Canada's national sport. This fast and exciting game played on an ice rink began in Canada in the mid-19th century and it is now played by many countries.

Ungava Peninsu

Hudson Bay

James Bay

Fort Albany

ONTARIO

Kenora

Timmins

Thunder Bay

Lake Superior

Sault Ste Marie

Lake Huron

Toronto ★

Kitchener

Lak On

Hamilton

Niagar Falls

Lake Michigan

London

Windsor

Lake Erie

0   200 miles

0   200 kilometers

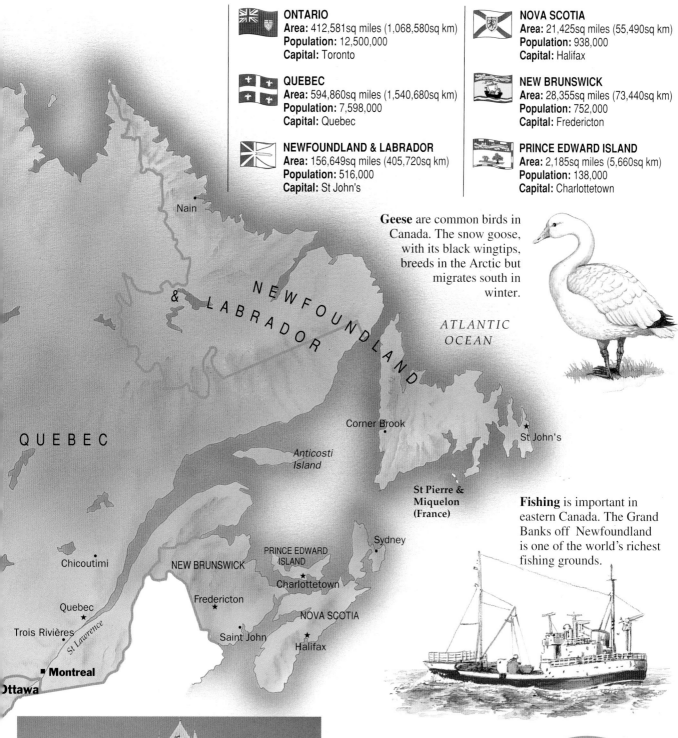

ONTARIO
Area: 412,581sq miles (1,068,580sq km)
Population: 12,500,000
Capital: Toronto

QUEBEC
Area: 594,860sq miles (1,540,680sq km)
Population: 7,598,000
Capital: Quebec

NEWFOUNDLAND & LABRADOR
Area: 156,649sq miles (405,720sq km)
Population: 516,000
Capital: St John's

NOVA SCOTIA
Area: 21,425sq miles (55,490sq km)
Population: 938,000
Capital: Halifax

NEW BRUNSWICK
Area: 28,355sq miles (73,440sq km)
Population: 752,000
Capital: Fredericton

PRINCE EDWARD ISLAND
Area: 2,185sq miles (5,660sq km)
Population: 138,000
Capital: Charlottetown

Geese are common birds in Canada. The snow goose, with its black wingtips, breeds in the Arctic but migrates south in winter.

Nain

N E W F O U N D L A N D
& L A B R A D O R

ATLANTIC OCEAN

QUEBEC

Corner Brook

St John's

Anticosti Island

St Pierre & Miquelon (France)

Fishing is important in eastern Canada. The Grand Banks off Newfoundland is one of the world's richest fishing grounds.

Sydney

PRINCE EDWARD ISLAND

Chicoutimi

NEW BRUNSWICK

Charlottetown

Fredericton

NOVA SCOTIA

Quebec

St Lawrence

Trois Rivières

Saint John

Halifax

Montreal

Ottawa

Quebec is Canada's oldest city and a major port. It was founded by Samuel de Champlain in 1608. Most of the people have French ancestors and many would like to make their province a separate French-speaking country.

WESTERN CANADA

Western Canada consists of four provinces – Alberta, British Columbia, Manitoba and Saskatchewan – and three territories – Northwest Territories, Nunavut, which was created in 1999, and Yukon Territory. The provinces contain vast plains called prairies, towering mountains in the west, and the Pacific coast. The three territories in the north are thinly populated. Less than one in a hundred Canadians lives there.

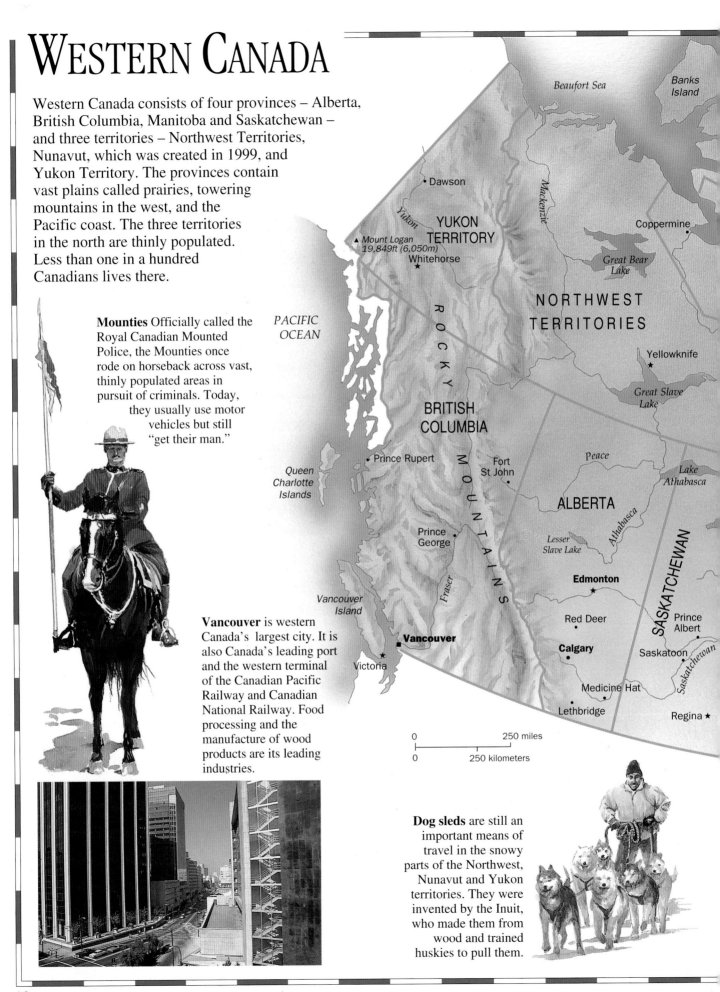

Mounties Officially called the Royal Canadian Mounted Police, the Mounties once rode on horseback across vast, thinly populated areas in pursuit of criminals. Today, they usually use motor vehicles but still "get their man."

Vancouver is western Canada's largest city. It is also Canada's leading port and the western terminal of the Canadian Pacific Railway and Canadian National Railway. Food processing and the manufacture of wood products are its leading industries.

Dog sleds are still an important means of travel in the snowy parts of the Northwest, Nunavut and Yukon territories. They were invented by the Inuit, who made them from wood and trained huskies to pull them.

Beaufort Sea

Banks Island

Dawson

Mackenzie

YUKON TERRITORY

Coppermine

▲ Mount Logan 19,849ft (6,050m)

Yukon

Whitehorse ★

Great Bear Lake

NORTHWEST TERRITORIES

PACIFIC OCEAN

Yellowknife ★

Great Slave Lake

R O C K Y

BRITISH COLUMBIA

Prince Rupert

Fort St John

Peace

Lake Athabasca

Queen Charlotte Islands

M O U N T A I N S

ALBERTA

Athabasca

SASKATCHEWAN

Prince George

Lesser Slave Lake

Edmonton ★

Fraser

Vancouver Island

Red Deer

Prince Albert

Vancouver ■

Calgary

Saskatoon

Victoria ★

Saskatchewan

Medicine Hat

Lethbridge

Regina ★

| 0 | | 250 miles |
| 0 | 250 kilometers | |

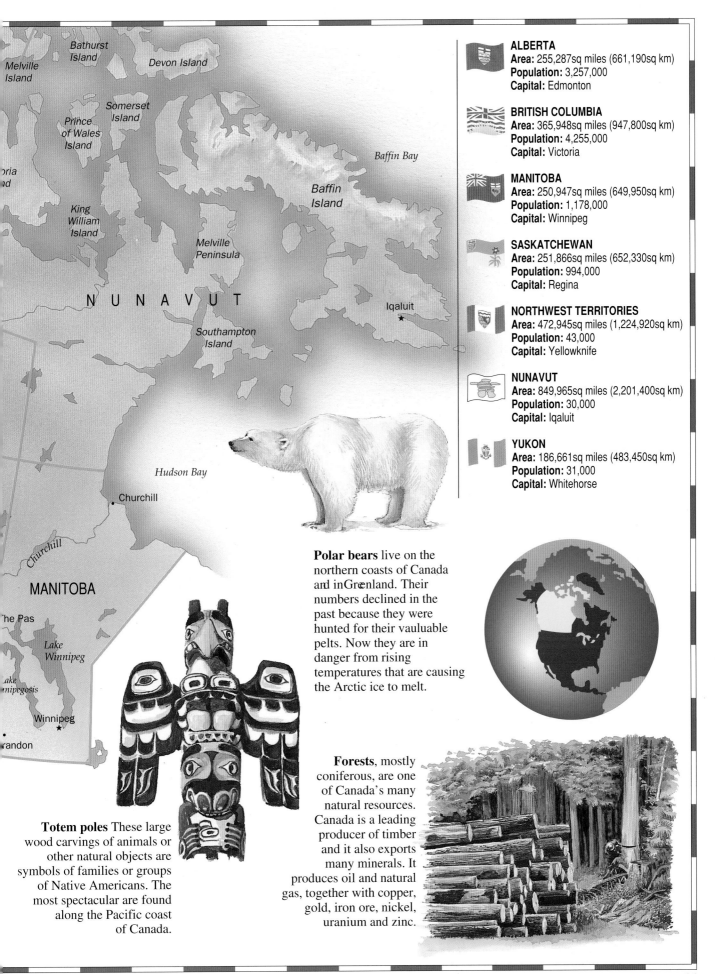

Melville
Island

Bathurst
Island

Devon Island

Somerset
Island

Prince
of Wales
Island

King
William
Island

oria
d

Baffin Bay

Baffin
Island

Melville
Peninsula

N U N A V U T

Iqaluit
★

Southampton
Island

Hudson Bay

Churchill

Churchill

MANITOBA

he Pas

Lake
Winnipeg

ake
nipegosis

Winnipeg
★

andon

ALBERTA
Area: 255,287sq miles (661,190sq km)
Population: 3,257,000
Capital: Edmonton

BRITISH COLUMBIA
Area: 365,948sq miles (947,800sq km)
Population: 4,255,000
Capital: Victoria

MANITOBA
Area: 250,947sq miles (649,950sq km)
Population: 1,178,000
Capital: Winnipeg

SASKATCHEWAN
Area: 251,866sq miles (652,330sq km)
Population: 994,000
Capital: Regina

NORTHWEST TERRITORIES
Area: 472,945sq miles (1,224,920sq km)
Population: 43,000
Capital: Yellowknife

NUNAVUT
Area: 849,965sq miles (2,201,400sq km)
Population: 30,000
Capital: Iqaluit

YUKON
Area: 186,661sq miles (483,450sq km)
Population: 31,000
Capital: Whitehorse

Polar bears live on the northern coasts of Canada and in Grenland. Their numbers declined in the past because they were hunted for their vauluable pelts. Now they are in danger from rising temperatures that are causing the Arctic ice to melt.

Totem poles These large wood carvings of animals or other natural objects are symbols of families or groups of Native Americans. The most spectacular are found along the Pacific coast of Canada.

Forests, mostly coniferous, are one of Canada's many natural resources. Canada is a leading producer of timber and it also exports many minerals. It produces oil and natural gas, together with copper, gold, iron ore, nickel, uranium and zinc.

UNITED STATES OF AMERICA

The United States is the world's fourth largest country but, in population, ranks third. The country consists of 50 states, 48 of which form a large block between Canada and Mexico. The 49th state, Alaska, lies in the far northwest of North America, while the 50th, Hawaii, is a chain of volcanic islands in the North Pacific Ocean. The United States also includes the District of Columbia, where the capital Washington, is located.

George Washington, the first president of the United States (1789-97), led the Continental Army against the British in the American War of Independence, or RevolutionaryWar, (1775-83). Its victory led to the birth of the United States.

Native Americans were the first people to live in what is now the United States. They crossed from Asia into North America at least 10,000 years ago.

Landscapes The United States has large forests, grasslands, snow-capped mountains and deserts. Much of the scenery is spectacular. Monument Valley on the Utah-Arizona border contains these remarkable rock formations.

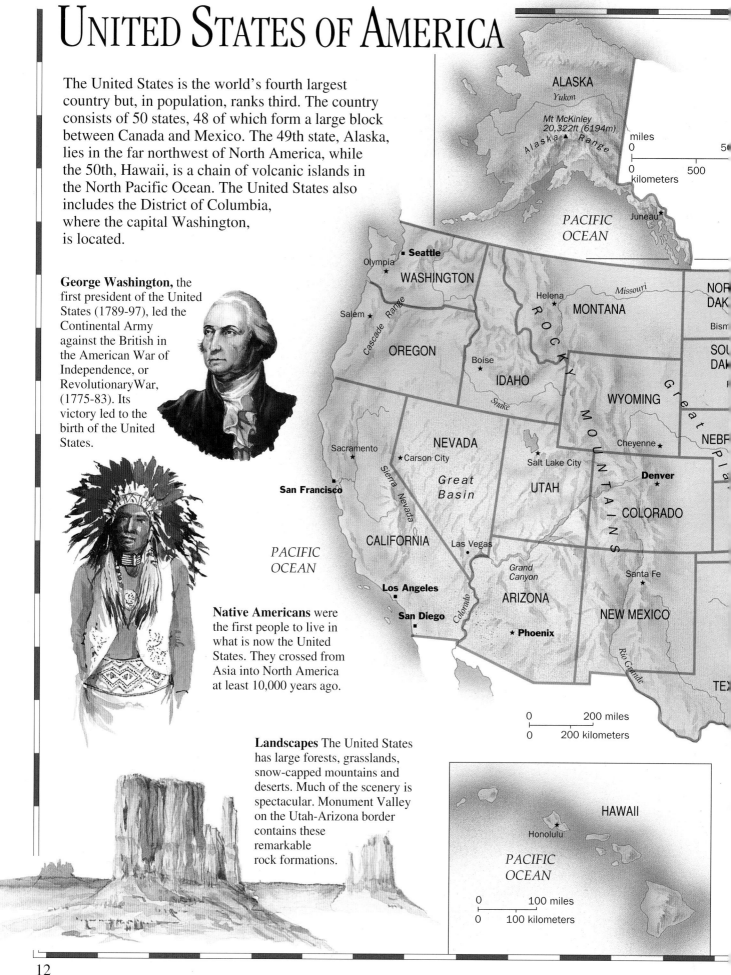

UNITED STATES

Capital: Washington, DC (pop 554,000)
Largest cities: New York City (8,104,000)
Los Angeles (3,846,000)
Chicago (2,862,000)
Official language: None (English is the chief
language spoken in the United States,
followed by Spanish)
Religions: Christianity (Protestant 52%,
Roman Catholic 24%, others 6%), Mormon 2%,
Judaism 1%, Islam 1%
Government: Federal republic
Currency: United States dollar

Area: 3,679,192sq miles
(9,529,063sq km)
Highest point: Mount McKinley,
20,322ft (6,194m)
Population: 298,444,000

Bald eagle This majestic bird of prey was adopted as the national bird in 1782. Overhunting, pollution and the destruction of wilderness areas threatened its survival, but it is now protected.

New York City The country's largest city has a magnificent skyline. The "9/11" attack on the World Trade Center, in which thousands lost their lives, destroyed the Twin Towers (top right).

Baseball is so popular that it has been called the national pastime of the United States. It was first played in the mid-18th century.

Exploring space Astronauts first landed on the moon in a lunar module like this in 1969. The United States is now using probes to explore Mars and the rest of the solar system.

MINNESOTA
St Paul
Lake Superior
MICHIGAN
Lake Huron
WISCONSIN
Lake Michigan
Madison **Milwaukee**
Lake Ontario
MAINE
Augusta
Montpelier
NEW HAMPSHIRE
VERMONT ★Concord
★ **Boston**
MASS. Providence
Albany★ Hartford★ R.I.
CONN.
Detroit
Lansing
Lake Erie
Chicago
Chicago
IOWA
Des Moines
ILLINOIS
Springfield
INDIANA
Indianapolis
OHIO
Columbus
Cincinnati
PENNSYLVANIA
Harrisburg★
★Trenton
New York City
NEW YORK
■**Philadelphia**
NEW JERSEY
★Dover
DELAWARE
Washington DC
Annapolis
MARYLAND
Kansas City
St Louis
WEST VIRGINIA
Ohio
VIRGINIA
Charleston★ ★Richmond
coln
eka★
MISSOURI
Jefferson City
★Frankfort
KENTUCKY
Nashville★
Tennessee
★Raleigh
NORTH CAROLINA
ATLANTIC OCEAN
SAS
KLAHOMA
lahoma City
ARKANSAS
Little Rock
TENNESSEE
Appalachian Mts
Columbia
SOUTH CAROLINA
★**Atlanta**
MISSISSIPPI
ALABAMA
GEORGIA
Montgomery
Jackson
★Tallahassee
Dallas
Red
Baton Rouge
stin
Houston
LOUISIANA
■**New Orleans**
FLORIDA
Antonio
Gulf of Mexico
●**Miami**
Mississippi

Northeastern States

The northeastern states region includes the six New England states of Connecticut, Maine, Massachusetts, New Hampshire, Rhode Island and Vermont. It also includes Delaware, Maryland, New Jersey, New York and Pennsylvania. The map also shows the country's capital, Washington, which lies within an area called the District of Columbia. The Northeast contains fertile farmland, great industrial cities and many historic sites.

New England is a historic region that formed part of the original 13 British colonies, which became the nucleus for the United States after the Revolutionary War of 1775-83. In the autumn New England's forests are ablaze with color.

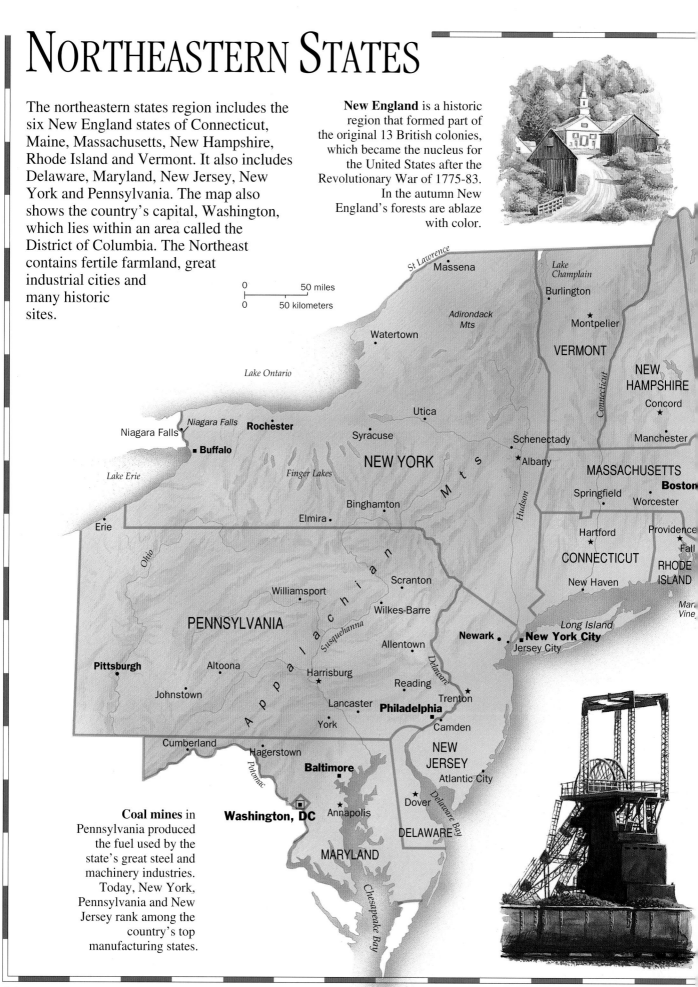

0   50 miles

0   50 kilometers

St Lawrence
Massena
Lake Champlain
Burlington
Adirondack Mts
Watertown
VERMONT
Montpelier ★
NEW HAMPSHIRE
Lake Ontario
Concord ★
Utica
Niagara Falls
Niagara Falls
Rochester
Syracuse
Schenectady
Manchester
Buffalo
NEW YORK
Albany ★
MASSACHUSETTS
Lake Erie
Finger Lakes
Springfield
Boston
Worcester
Binghamton
Hartford ★
Providence ★
Elmira
Erie
Ohio
CONNECTICUT
Fall
Mts
Hudson
New Haven
RHODE ISLAND
Scranton
Mar Vine
Williamsport
Wilkes-Barre
Long Island
Newark
New York City
Jersey City
PENNSYLVANIA
Susquehanna
Allentown
Altoona
Pittsburgh
Harrisburg ★
Reading
Appalachian
Delaware
Johnstown
Lancaster
Trenton ★
York
Philadelphia
Camden
Cumberland
NEW JERSEY
Hagerstown
Atlantic City
Potomac
Baltimore
Dover ★
Washington, DC
Annapolis ★
Delaware Bay
DELAWARE
MARYLAND
Chesapeake Bay

Coal mines in Pennsylvania produced the fuel used by the state's great steel and machinery industries. Today, New York, Pennsylvania and New Jersey rank among the country's top manufacturing states.

Presque Isle

Moosehead Lake

MAINE

Bangor

ugusta

ATLANTIC OCEAN

land

e Cod

Nantucket Island

Capitol This is the building in Washington, DC, where Congress (the Senate and the House of Representatives) meets. President George Washington laid its cornerstone in 1793 and Congress first met there in 1800.

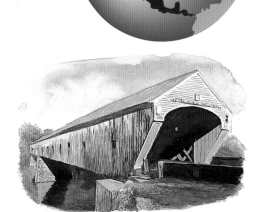

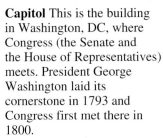

Covered bridges have a roof and sides that protect the wooden structure from the weather. The first long covered bridge in the United States was built in Massachusetts in 1806.

Abraham Lincoln served as president of the United States between 1860 and 1865, when he was assassinated. He led the nation during the Civil War (1861-65).

Liberty Bell This church bell in Philadelphia is a symbol of American freedom. It was rung on July 8, 1776, to announce the adoption of the Declaration of Independence. The bell broke in 1835 and is no longer rung.

 CONNECTICUT
Area: 5,018sq miles (12,997sq km)
Population: 3,504,000
Capital: Hartford

 DELAWARE
Area: 2,045sq miles (5,294sq km)
Population: 830,000
Capital: Dover

 MAINE
Area: 33,265sq miles (86,156sq km)
Population: 1,317,000
Capital: Augusta

 MARYLAND
Area: 10,460sq miles (27,091sq km)
Population: 5,558,000
Capital: Annapolis

 MASSACHUSETTS
Area: 8,284sq miles (21,455sq km)
Population: 6,417,000
Capital: Boston

 NEW HAMPSHIRE
Area: 9,279sq miles (24,032sq km)
Population: 1,300,000
Capital: Concord

 NEW JERSEY
Area: 7,787sq miles (20,168sq km)
Population: 8,699,000
Capital: Trenton

 NEW YORK
Area: 52,735sq miles (136,583sq km)
Population: 19,227,000
Capital: Albany

 PENNSYLVANIA
Area: 46,043sq miles (119,251sq km)
Population: 12,408,000
Capital: Harrisburg

 RHODE ISLAND
Area: 1,212sq miles (3,139sq km)
Population: 1,081,000
Capital: Providence

 VERMONT
Area: 9,614sq miles (24,900sq km)
Population: 621,000
Capital: Montpelier

 DISTRICT OF COLUMBIA
Area: 69sq miles (179sq km)
Population: 554,000

SOUTHEASTERN STATES

The southeastern states contain large areas of coastal plains and the southern part of the scenic Appalachian Mountains. The region is rich in history. Virginia, North and South Carolina and Georgia were among the 13 English colonies that formed the nucleus of the United States, while the region also played a major part in the Civil War. The states once depended on farming, but manufacturing is now important.

Coca-Cola is regarded as a symbol of American taste all over the world. It was first produced by a pharmacist, John S. Pemberton, in Atlanta in 1886. The Coca-Cola Company, founded in 1892, keeps secret the ingredients used in the drink.

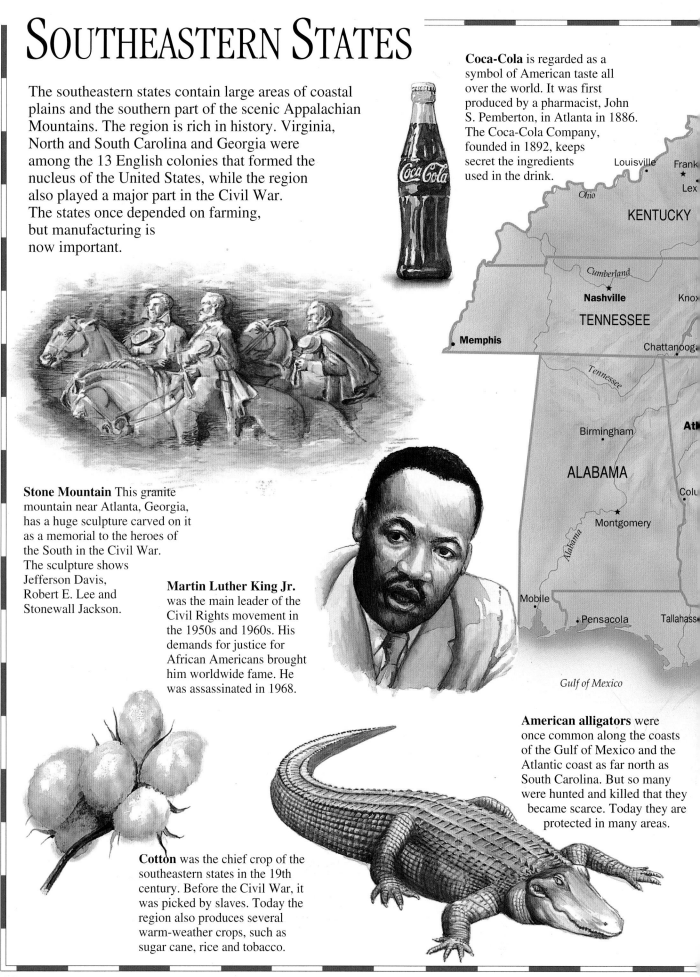

Stone Mountain This granite mountain near Atlanta, Georgia, has a huge sculpture carved on it as a memorial to the heroes of the South in the Civil War. The sculpture shows Jefferson Davis, Robert E. Lee and Stonewall Jackson.

Martin Luther King Jr. was the main leader of the Civil Rights movement in the 1950s and 1960s. His demands for justice for African Americans brought him worldwide fame. He was assassinated in 1968.

American alligators were once common along the coasts of the Gulf of Mexico and the Atlantic coast as far north as South Carolina. But so many were hunted and killed that they became scarce. Today they are protected in many areas.

Cotton was the chief crop of the southeastern states in the 19th century. Before the Civil War, it was picked by slaves. Today the region also produces several warm-weather crops, such as sugar cane, rice and tobacco.

Louisville
Frank
Ohio
Lex
KENTUCKY
Cumberland
Nashville
Knox
TENNESSEE
Memphis
Chattanoog
Tennessee
Atl
Birmingham
ALABAMA
Col
Montgomery
Alabama
Mobile
Pensacola
Tallahass
Gulf of Mexico

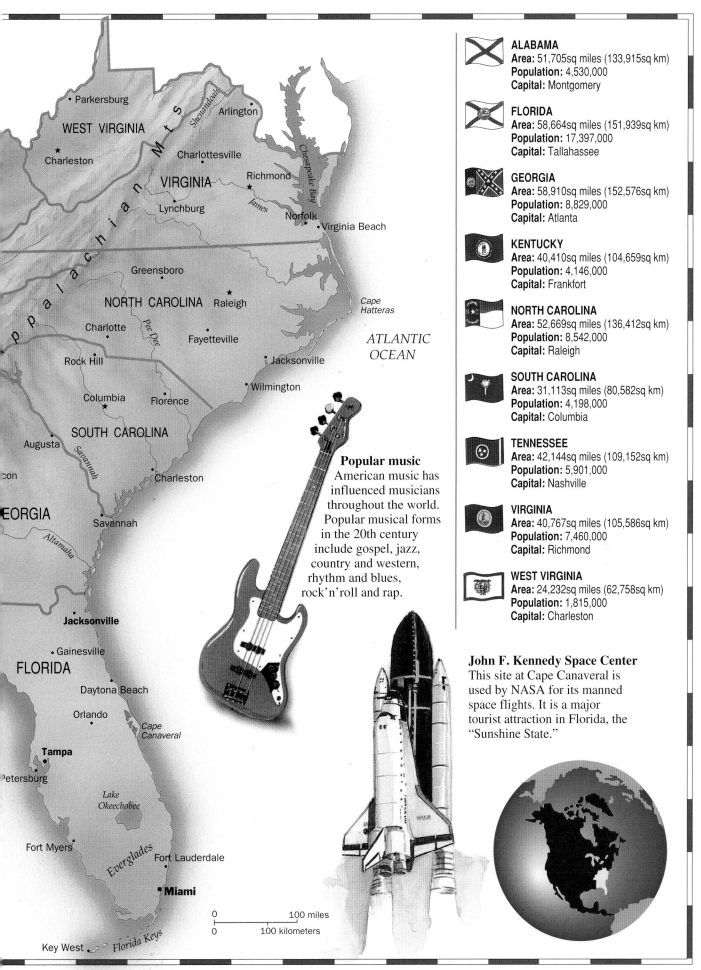

Parkersburg

WEST VIRGINIA

Charleston ★

Arlington

Shenandoah

Charlottesville

Richmond ★

VIRGINIA

Lynchburg

James

Norfolk

Virginia Beach

Chesapeake Bay

Greensboro

NORTH CAROLINA   Raleigh ★

Charlotte

Pee Dee

Fayetteville

Cape
Hatteras

Rock Hill

Jacksonville

ATLANTIC
OCEAN

Columbia ★

Florence

Wilmington

SOUTH CAROLINA

Augusta

Savannah

Charleston

con

EORGIA

Savannah

Altamaha

Jacksonville

Gainesville

FLORIDA

Daytona Beach

Orlando

Cape
Canaveral

Tampa

etersburg

*Lake
Okeechobee*

Fort Myers

Everglades

Fort Lauderdale

Miami

Key West

Florida Keys

0   100 miles
0   100 kilometers

ALABAMA
Area: 51,705sq miles (133,915sq km)
Population: 4,530,000
Capital: Montgomery

FLORIDA
Area: 58,664sq miles (151,939sq km)
Population: 17,397,000
Capital: Tallahassee

GEORGIA
Area: 58,910sq miles (152,576sq km)
Population: 8,829,000
Capital: Atlanta

KENTUCKY
Area: 40,410sq miles (104,659sq km)
Population: 4,146,000
Capital: Frankfort

NORTH CAROLINA
Area: 52,669sq miles (136,412sq km)
Population: 8,542,000
Capital: Raleigh

SOUTH CAROLINA
Area: 31,113sq miles (80,582sq km)
Population: 4,198,000
Capital: Columbia

TENNESSEE
Area: 42,144sq miles (109,152sq km)
Population: 5,901,000
Capital: Nashville

VIRGINIA
Area: 40,767sq miles (105,586sq km)
Population: 7,460,000
Capital: Richmond

WEST VIRGINIA
Area: 24,232sq miles (62,758sq km)
Population: 1,815,000
Capital: Charleston

Popular music
American music has
influenced musicians
throughout the world.
Popular musical forms
in the 20th century
include gospel, jazz,
country and western,
rhythm and blues,
rock'n'roll and rap.

John F. Kennedy Space Center
This site at Cape Canaveral is
used by NASA for its manned
space flights. It is a major
tourist attraction in Florida, the
"Sunshine State."

17

SOUTH-CENTRAL STATES

Arkansas, Louisiana and Mississippi, which form the eastern part of the south-central states, are drained by the Mississippi River valley. In the west lie the vast open spaces of Texas and Oklahoma. These two states, together with Louisiana, are among the top five petroleum producers in the United States. The region also contains some major cities, including Houston, San Antonio and Dallas, which are among the country's top ten cities.

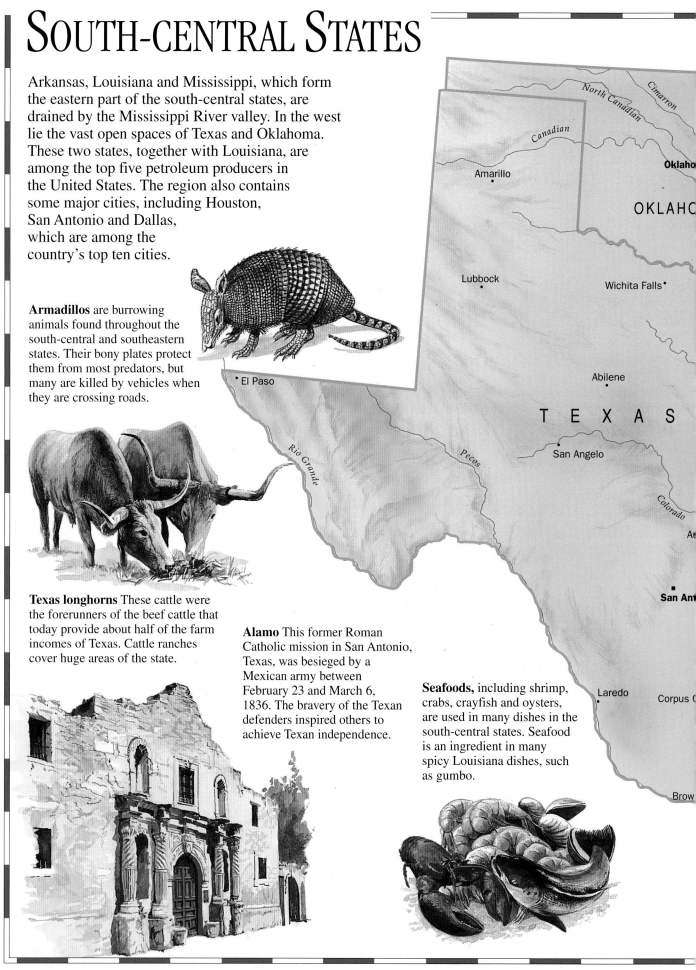

Armadillos are burrowing animals found throughout the south-central and southeastern states. Their bony plates protect them from most predators, but many are killed by vehicles when they are crossing roads.

Texas longhorns These cattle were the forerunners of the beef cattle that today provide about half of the farm incomes of Texas. Cattle ranches cover huge areas of the state.

Alamo This former Roman Catholic mission in San Antonio, Texas, was besieged by a Mexican army between February 23 and March 6, 1836. The bravery of the Texan defenders inspired others to achieve Texan independence.

Seafoods, including shrimp, crabs, crayfish and oysters, are used in many dishes in the south-central states. Seafood is an ingredient in many spicy Louisiana dishes, such as gumbo.

Amarillo

Oklaho

OKLAHO

Lubbock

Wichita Falls

El Paso

Abilene

T E X A S

San Angelo

Pecos

Colorado

At

San An

Laredo

Corpus C

Brow

North Canadian

Cimarron

Canadian

Rio Grande

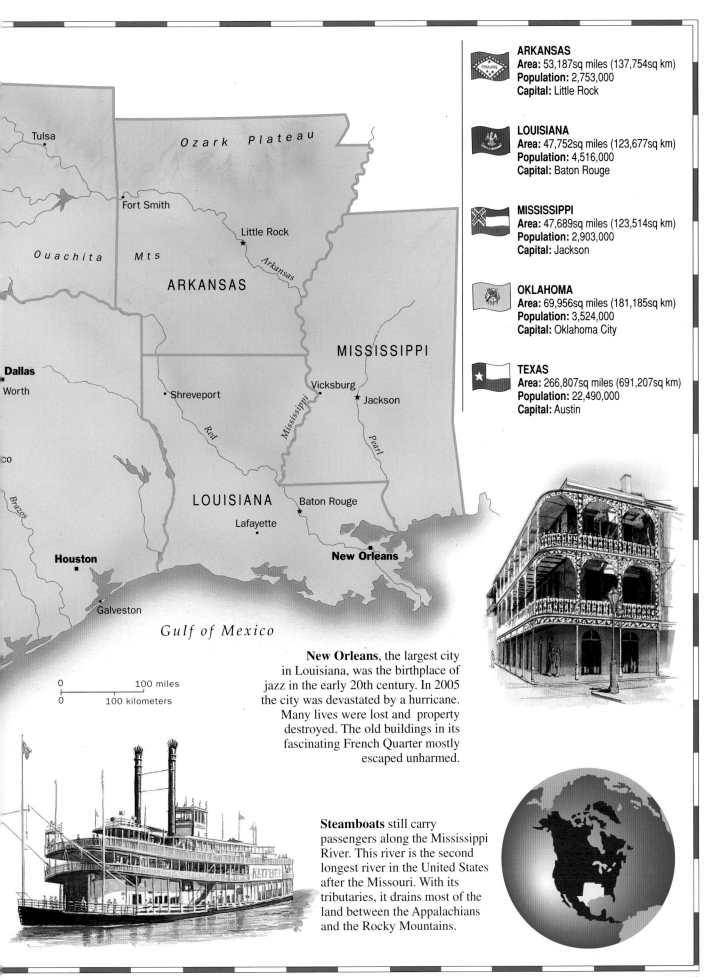

ARKANSAS
Area: 53,187sq miles (137,754sq km)
Population: 2,753,000
Capital: Little Rock

LOUISIANA
Area: 47,752sq miles (123,677sq km)
Population: 4,516,000
Capital: Baton Rouge

MISSISSIPPI
Area: 47,689sq miles (123,514sq km)
Population: 2,903,000
Capital: Jackson

OKLAHOMA
Area: 69,956sq miles (181,185sq km)
Population: 3,524,000
Capital: Oklahoma City

TEXAS
Area: 266,807sq miles (691,207sq km)
Population: 22,490,000
Capital: Austin

Tulsa

Ozark   Plateau

Fort Smith

Little Rock

Ouachita   Mts

ARKANSAS

Arkansas

Dallas
Worth

MISSISSIPPI

Shreveport

Vicksburg

Jackson

Mississippi

Red

Pearl

LOUISIANA

Baton Rouge

Lafayette

Brazos

Houston

New Orleans

Galveston

Gulf of Mexico

```
0              100 miles
0         100 kilometers
```

New Orleans, the largest city in Louisiana, was the birthplace of jazz in the early 20th century. In 2005 the city was devastated by a hurricane. Many lives were lost and property destroyed. The old buildings in its fascinating French Quarter mostly escaped unharmed.

Steamboats still carry passengers along the Mississippi River. This river is the second longest river in the United States after the Missouri. With its tributaries, it drains most of the land between the Appalachians and the Rocky Mountains.

MIDWESTERN STATES

The 12 midwestern states cover about a fifth of the United States. The land is mostly flat, including parts of the Great Plains in the west and the lower Interior Plains south and west of the Great Lakes. Farmers produce grains and other crops on the fertile land, together with dairy products and livestock. Major industrial cities include Chicago, Detroit and Indianapolis. The Great Lakes and the Mississippi River are used to transport goods.

Bison once roamed the Midwest in huge herds, but hunters slaughtered most of them. Today a few thousand live in protected areas.

Mount Rushmore National Memorial, in South Dakota, is a carving of four presidents: George Washington, Thomas Jefferson,Theodore Roosevelt and Abraham Lincoln. Each face is about 60ft (18m) high.

Football is played by university and college teams. The professional National Football League is divided into the American Football Conference and the National Football Conference.

Pioneers had reached the Mississippi by the 1820s. In the 1840s wagon trains crossed the Great Plains and, by the 1890s, scattered settlements had sprung up all across this dry region.

NORTH DAKOTA

Red Lake

Lake Sakakawea

Bismarck ★

Fargo •

Duluth •

MINNESOTA

Great Plains

Minneapolis • ★ St Paul

SOUTH DAKOTA

Pierre ★　Lake Oahe

Black Hills

▲ Mt Rushmore

Sioux Falls •

Missouri

• Sioux City

Cedar R

IOWA

★ Des Moines

NEBRASKA

Platte

Omaha •

Lincoln ★

Kansas

■ Kansas City

★ Topeka

KANSAS

Jefferson ★

MISSO

Wichita •

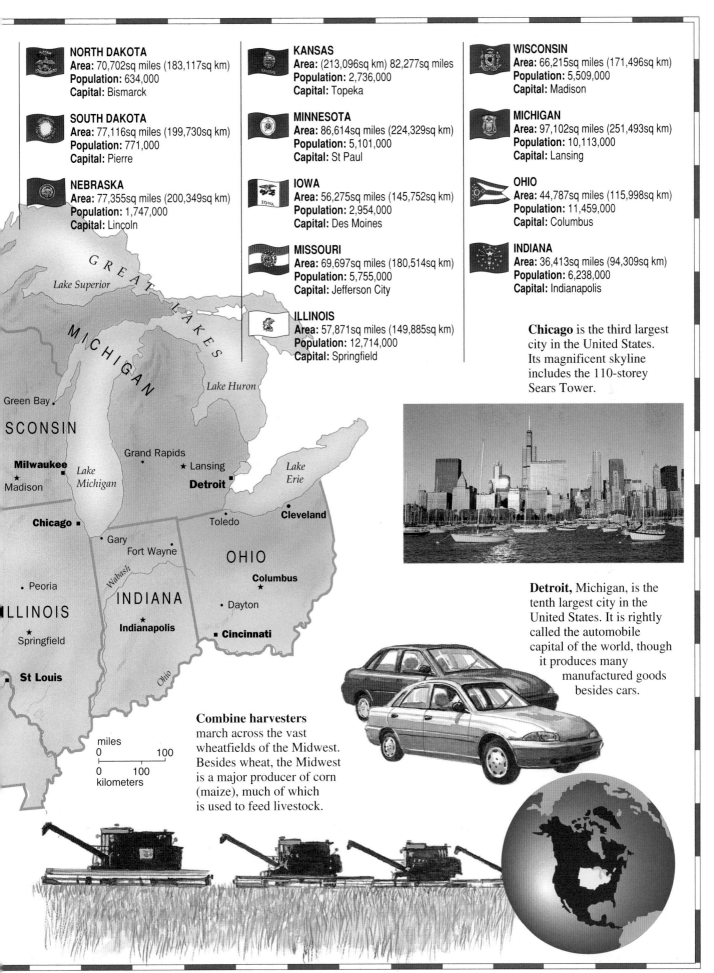

NORTH DAKOTA
Area: 70,702sq miles (183,117sq km)
Population: 634,000
Capital: Bismarck

SOUTH DAKOTA
Area: 77,116sq miles (199,730sq km)
Population: 771,000
Capital: Pierre

NEBRASKA
Area: 77,355sq miles (200,349sq km)
Population: 1,747,000
Capital: Lincoln

KANSAS
Area: (213,096sq km) 82,277sq miles
Population: 2,736,000
Capital: Topeka

MINNESOTA
Area: 86,614sq miles (224,329sq km)
Population: 5,101,000
Capital: St Paul

IOWA
Area: 56,275sq miles (145,752sq km)
Population: 2,954,000
Capital: Des Moines

MISSOURI
Area: 69,697sq miles (180,514sq km)
Population: 5,755,000
Capital: Jefferson City

ILLINOIS
Area: 57,871sq miles (149,885sq km)
Population: 12,714,000
Capital: Springfield

WISCONSIN
Area: 66,215sq miles (171,496sq km)
Population: 5,509,000
Capital: Madison

MICHIGAN
Area: 97,102sq miles (251,493sq km)
Population: 10,113,000
Capital: Lansing

OHIO
Area: 44,787sq miles (115,998sq km)
Population: 11,459,000
Capital: Columbus

INDIANA
Area: 36,413sq miles (94,309sq km)
Population: 6,238,000
Capital: Indianapolis

Chicago is the third largest city in the United States. Its magnificent skyline includes the 110-storey Sears Tower.

Detroit, Michigan, is the tenth largest city in the United States. It is rightly called the automobile capital of the world, though it produces many manufactured goods besides cars.

Combine harvesters march across the vast wheatfields of the Midwest. Besides wheat, the Midwest is a major producer of corn (maize), much of which is used to feed livestock.

miles
0   100
0   100
kilometers

NORTHWESTERN STATES

The eastern part of the northwestern states is part of the flat Great Plains. But the west is largely mountainous. The Cascade Range in Oregon and Washington has active volcanoes including Mount Saint Helens, which exploded with great force in 1980, killing 57 people. Alaska, which became the 49th state on January 3, 1959, also has active volcanoes. Alaska is rich in oil, while farming and forestry are important in the other five states.

Aircraft are made by the Boeing Company, which has its headquarters in Seattle. The city is also the home of Microsoft, the world's leading computer software company. The manufacture of wood products and processed foods are other major industries in the Northwest.

Mount McKinley, in south-central Alaska, is the highest mountain in North America. It got its name from William McKinley who was US President from 1897-1901. Its Native American name Denali means "The Great One."

Grizzly bears roam the forests of Alaska and western Canada. Some also live in remote areas of the northwestern states, but many of the places where the bears once lived are now occupied by people.

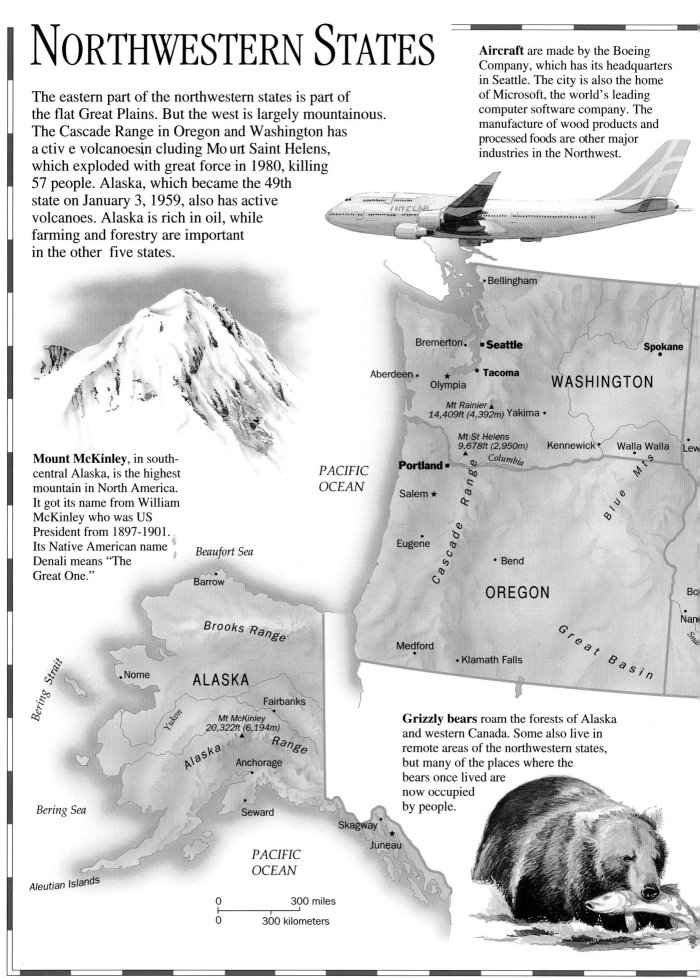

PACIFIC OCEAN

• Bellingham

Bremerton • ■ **Seattle**   **Spokane**

Aberdeen •   ★   • **Tacoma**   **WASHINGTON**
              Olympia
                   Mt Rainier ▲   Yakima •
                   14,409ft (4,392m)

                   Mt St Helens
                   9,678ft (2,950m)   Kennewick •   Walla Walla   Lew
Portland ■   ▲
                        Columbia
Salem ★   Blue Mts

                                    Cascade Range
Eugene •
                        • Bend

                                    OREGON   Bo

Medford •   Nan
        • Klamath Falls   Great Basin   Sna

Beaufort Sea

Barrow

Brooks Range

Bering Strait

• Nome   **ALASKA**

                        Fairbanks •
        Yukon   Mt McKinley
                 20,322ft (6,194m) ▲   Range
                                Alaska
Bering Sea   Anchorage •

                        • Seward

                                    Skagway •
PACIFIC   ★
OCEAN   Juneau

Aleutian Islands

0 _____ 300 miles
0 _____ 300 kilometers

22

ALASKA
Area: 591,004sq miles
(1,530,693sq km)
Population: 655,000
Capital: Juneau

IDAHO
Area: 83,564sq miles (216,430sq km)
Population: 1,393,000
Capital: Boise

MONTANA
Area: 147,046sq miles (380,849sq km)
Population: 927,000
Capital: Helena

OREGON
Area: 97,073sq miles (251,418sq km)
Population: 3,595,000
Capital: Salem

WASHINGTON
Area: 68,139sq miles (176,479sq km)
Population: 6,204,000
Capital: Olympia

WYOMING
Area: 97,809sq miles (253,324sq km)
Population: 507,000
Capital: Cheyenne

Native Americans in the Northwest fished and hunted animals. They also gathered plant foods in the forests. They used wood to build houses and boats, and to make containers, bowls, utensils and masks like this one.

Yellowstone National Park lies mainly in northwestern Wyoming. It was set up in 1872 and is the world's oldest national park. It contains hot springs and geysers, canyons and huge waterfalls.

0   100 miles

0   100 kilometers

Devils Tower, in northeastern Wyoming, is a mountain formed from hard volcanic rock. It rises 865ft (264m) from its base. It became the country's first national monument in 1906.

SOUTHWESTERN STATES

The southwestern states contain much magnificent scenery. California has more people than any other state and is the country's leading manufacturing and farming state. It also has valuable mineral deposits, including oil and natural gas. If California were a separate country, it would rank among the world's top ten in terms of the total value of the goods and services it produces. Hawaii, in the Pacific Ocean, became the 50th state on August 21, 1959.

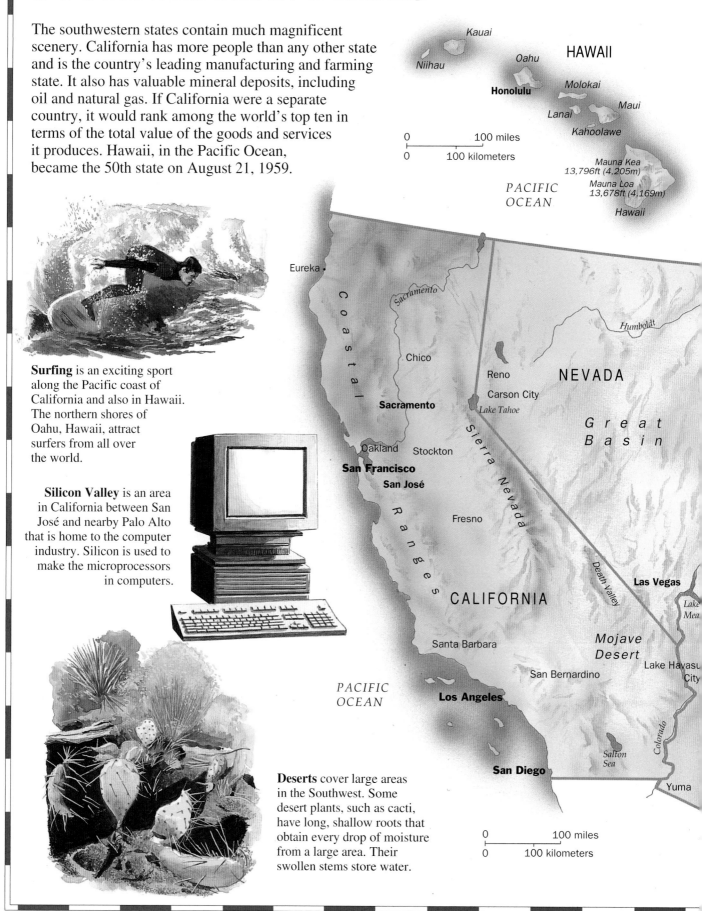

Surfing is an exciting sport along the Pacific coast of California and also in Hawaii. The northern shores of Oahu, Hawaii, attract surfers from all over the world.

Silicon Valley is an area in California between San José and nearby Palo Alto that is home to the computer industry. Silicon is used to make the microprocessors in computers.

Deserts cover large areas in the Southwest. Some desert plants, such as cacti, have long, shallow roots that obtain every drop of moisture from a large area. Their swollen stems store water.

HAWAII

Kauai
Niihau
Oahu
Honolulu
Molokai
Lanai
Maui
Kahoolawe
Mauna Kea 13,796ft (4,205m)
Mauna Loa 13,678ft (4,169m)
Hawaii

PACIFIC OCEAN

0 — 100 miles
0 — 100 kilometers

Eureka
Coastal
Sacramento
Chico
Reno
Carson City
Lake Tahoe
NEVADA
Humboldt
Great Basin
Sacramento
Oakland
Stockton
San Francisco
San José
Sierra Nevada
Fresno
Ranges
Death Valley
Las Vegas
CALIFORNIA
Lake Mead
Santa Barbara
Mojave Desert
San Bernardino
Lake Havasu City
PACIFIC OCEAN
Los Angeles
Colorado
Salton Sea
San Diego
Yuma

0 — 100 miles
0 — 100 kilometers

Kilauea is an active volcano on the eastern slope of Mauna Loa, Hawaii. It emits runny lava that flows down to the sea. All of the islands in Hawaii were formed by volcanoes. But only the volcanoes on Hawaii itself are active. The others are extinct.

Grand Canyon This huge canyon was carved out by the Colorado River and is around 1 mile (1.6km) deep in places. The canyon, like many of the country's scenic wonders, is protected in a national park.

ARIZONA
Area: 114,000sq miles (295,259sq km)
Population: 5,744,000
Capital: Phoenix

CALIFORNIA
Area: 158,706sq miles (411,047sq km)
Population: 35,894,000
Capital: Sacramento

COLORADO
Area: 104,091sq miles (269,594sq km)
Population: 4,601,000
Capital: Denver

HAWAII
Area: 6,471sq miles (16,760sq km)
Population: 1,263,000
Capital: Honolulu

NEVADA
Area: 110,561sq miles (286,352sq km)
Population: 2,335,000
Capital: Carson City

NEW MEXICO
Area: 121,593sq miles (314,924sq km)
Population: 1,903,000
Capital: Santa Fe

UTAH
Area: 84,899sq miles (219,887sq km)
Population: 2,389,000
Capital: Salt Lake City

Mesa Verde is a national park in southwestern Colorado. Its name means "green table" and it contains impressive remains of cliff dwellings built by Native Americans hundreds of years ago.

MEXICO

Mexico, the third largest country in North America, forms a bridge between the United States and the seven countries of Central America. The land is mainly mountainous, with deserts in the north and rainforests in the south. Temperatures vary according to the height of the land. Farming is important, but Mexico's main exports are oil and oil products. Factories in the north assemble goods, such as vehicle parts, for US companies.

MEXICO

Area: 761,605sq miles (1,972,547sq km)
Highest point: Citlaltépetl (also called Orizaba), 18,701ft (5,700m)
Population: 107,450,000
Capital and largest city: Mexico City (pop 18,660,000)
Other large cities: Guadalajara (3,697,000) Monterrey (3,267,000) Puebla (1,888,000)
Official language: Spanish
Religion: Christianity (Roman Catholic 89%, Protestant 5%, other 5%)
Government: Federal republic
Currency: Mexican peso

Monarch butterfly This colorful creature holds the record among insects for the distance it migrates each year. In autumn, it travels from New England to the southern United States and Mexico. In spring it returns to the north.

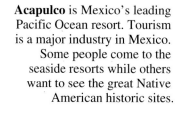

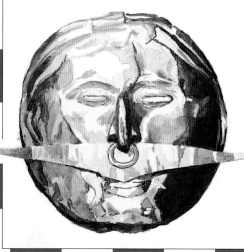

Tarantula is the popular name given to large hairy bird-eating spiders of the family Theraphosidae, which are found between the southwestern United States and South America. They look frightening but their bit is generally not serious.

Tijuana Mexicali Colorado

Ciudad Juárez

Hermosillo

Chihuahua

Baja California Gulf of California Sierra Madre Occiden

Culiacán

La Paz

Dur

Mazatlán

PACIFIC OCEAN

Acapulco is Mexico's leading Pacific Ocean resort. Tourism is a major industry in Mexico. Some people come to the seaside resorts while others want to see the great Native American historic sites.

Gold and silver objects made by Aztecs are evidence of their artistic skills. According to legend, the Aztec capital, Tenochtitlán, was founded in 1325. The Aztecs were defeated by Spanish soldiers in 1521.

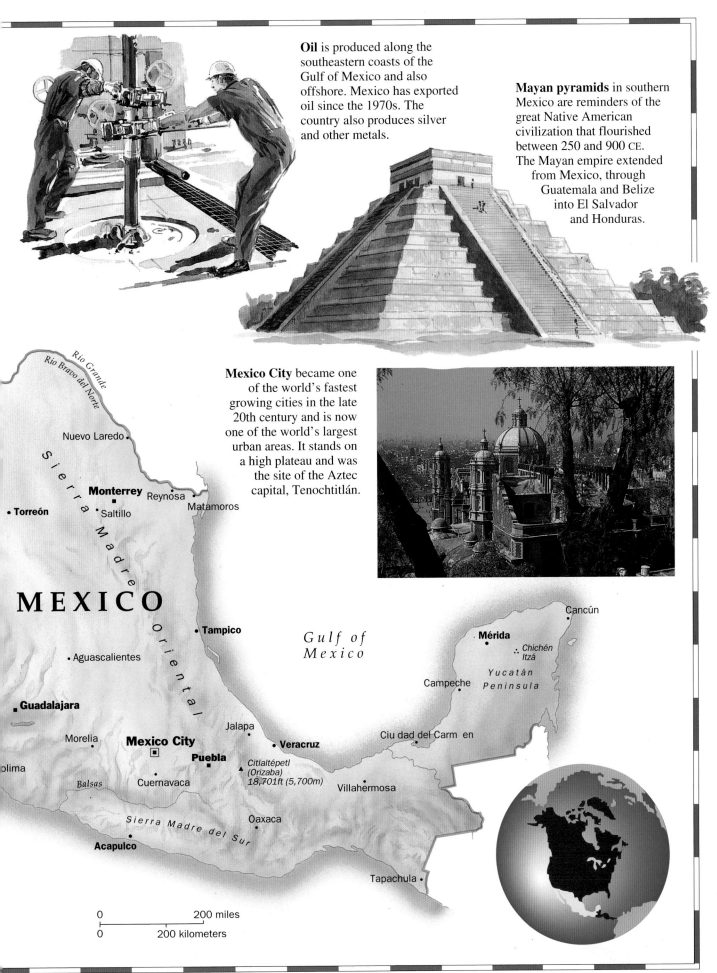

Oil is produced along the southeastern coasts of the Gulf of Mexico and also offshore. Mexico has exported oil since the 1970s. The country also produces silver and other metals.

Mayan pyramids in southern Mexico are reminders of the great Native American civilization that flourished between 250 and 900 CE. The Mayan empire extended from Mexico, through Guatemala and Belize into El Salvador and Honduras.

Mexico City became one of the world's fastest growing cities in the late 20th century and is now one of the world's largest urban areas. It stands on a high plateau and was the site of the Aztec capital, Tenochtitlán.

Rio Grande
Rio Bravo del Norte

Sierra Madre Oriental

Nuevo Laredo

Monterrey Reynosa

• Torreón • Saltillo Matamoros

MEXICO

• Tampico

• Aguascalientes

• Guadalajara

Morelia

Mexico City
□

Puebla
■

olima

Balsas Cuernavaca

Jalapa **• Veracruz**

Citlaltépetl (Orizaba)
18,701ft (5,700m)

Villahermosa

Sierra Madre del Sur

Oaxaca

Acapulco

Tapachula

Gulf of Mexico

Cancún

Mérida
• ∴ Chichén Itzá

Yucatán Peninsula

Campeche

Ciu dad del Carm en

0 ————— 200 miles
0 ————— 200 kilometers

WESTERN CENTRAL AMERICA

Western Central America consists of four countries: Belize, El Salvador, Guatemala and Honduras. Hot and humid coasts border the region in the north and south. Between lies a highland zone with many active volcanoes. The people include Native Americans, together with people of African and European descent. Many people are of mixed origin. Farming is the main activity. Most people live in the cooler highlands.

Coral reefs and islands stretch along the swampy coast of Belize. They form the world's second longest barrier reef after Australia's Great Barrier Reef and they are an important breeding area for fish.

BELIZE

Area: 8,867sq miles (22,965sq km)
Population: 287,000
Capital: Belmopan (pop 9,000)
Largest city: Belize City (50,000)
Government: Constitutional monarchy
Official language: English
Currency: Belize dollar

EL SALVADOR

Area: 8,124 sq miles (21,041sq km)
Population: 6,822,000
Capital and largest city: San Salvador (pop 1,424,000)
Government: Republic
Official language: Spanish
Currency: US dollar

GUATEMALA

Area: 42,042sq miles (108,889sq km)
Population: 12,294,000
Capital and largest city: Guatemala City (pop 951,000)
Government: Republic
Official language: Spanish
Currency: Quetzal, US dollar

HONDURAS

Area: 43,277sq miles (112,088sq km)
Population: 7,326,000
Capital and largest city: Tegucigalpa (pop 1,007,000)
Government: Republic
Official language: Spanish
Currency: Lempira

0   50 miles
0   50 kilometers

Belize
Tikal
Belmopan
BELIZE
Chixoy
Puerto Barrio
GUATEMALA
Lake Izabal
▲ Tajumulco 13,812ft (4,210m)
Motagua
Quezaltenango
Guatemala City
Mazatenango
Antigua
Santa Ana
PACIFIC OCEAN
Sonsonate
San Salvador
EL SALVADOR

Coffee is grown in the highlands of Central America and most of the berries on the coffee plants are hand picked. Coffee is the chief export of El Salvador, Guatemala and Honduras.

Tikal, in northern Guatemala, contains huge ruined pyramids. It was the biggest city of the Maya. Its main temple stood on top of a pyramid 150ft (45m) tall.

Bananas grow well in hot, wet climates and they are a leading crop on the lowlands of Central America. The other main crop grown for export in lowland areas is sugar cane.

Caribbean Sea

Gulf of Honduras

Islas de la Bahía

Tela

La Ceiba

Pedro Sula

Patuca

Juticalpa

HONDURAS

Tegucigalpa

iguel

Manatees, or sea cows, live along the Caribbean coasts of Central America and northern South America. Found in sheltered coastal waters, they have suffered from the effects of pollution and the use of power boats.

Market days in Guatemalan towns and villages are lively occasions, when farmers bring their products for sale. About one-third of Guatemala's people are direct descendants of the original Native Americans.

EASTERN CENTRAL AMERICA

Like western Central America, Costa Rica, Nicaragua and Panama have hot, tropical climates except in highland areas which are cooler. Nicaragua is the largest country in Central America. Like Costa Rica, it lies in an unstable area where earthquakes and volcanic eruptions are common. Costa Rica has many beautiful national parks and now attracts many tourists. Panama is an isthmus, a narrow strip of land linking North and South America.

 **COSTA RICA**

Area: 19,575sq miles (50,700sq km)
Population: 4,075,000
Capital and largest city: San José
(pop 1,085,000)
Government: Republic
Official language: Spanish
Religions: Christianity (Roman Catholic 76%)
Currency: Costa Rican colón

NICARAGUA

Area: 50,193sq miles (130,000sq km)
Population: 5,570,000
Capital and largest city: Managua
(pop 1,098,000)
Government: Republic
Official language: Spanish
Religions: Christianity (Roman Catholic 73%)
Currency: Córdoba

PANAMA

Area: 29,762sq miles (77,082sq km)
Population: 3,191,000
Capital and largest city: Panama City
(pop 930,000)
Government: Republic
Official language: Spanish
Religions: Christianity (Roman Catholic 85%)
Currency: Balboa

Pan-American Highway
This road system extends through the Americas from the United States border to southern Chile. The only break is in Panama where the route is blocked by dense rainforest.

Active volcanoes Volcanic eruptions are common throughout the highlands of Nicaragua and Costa Rica. The volcanic rocks have weathered to produce rich, fertile soils.

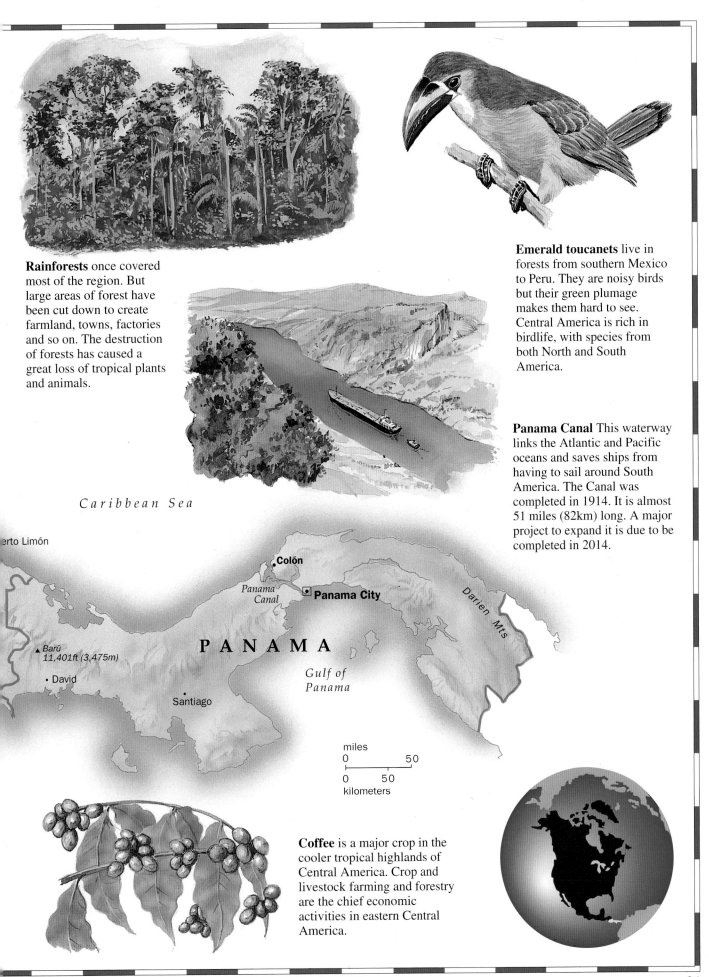

Rainforests once covered most of the region. But large areas of forest have been cut down to create farmland, towns, factories and so on. The destruction of forests has caused a great loss of tropical plants and animals.

Emerald toucanets live in forests from southern Mexico to Peru. They are noisy birds but their green plumage makes them hard to see. Central America is rich in birdlife, with species from both North and South America.

Panama Canal This waterway links the Atlantic and Pacific oceans and saves ships from having to sail around South America. The Canal was completed in 1914. It is almost 51 miles (82km) long. A major project to expand it is due to be completed in 2014.

Caribbean Sea

erto Limón

Colón

Panama Canal

□ **Panama City**

Darien Mts

P A N A M A

▲ *Barú*
11,401ft (3,475m)

• David

Gulf of Panama

Santiago

miles
0 _____ 50

0 ___ 50
kilometers

Coffee is a major crop in the cooler tropical highlands of Central America. Crop and livestock farming and forestry are the chief economic activities in eastern Central America.

Northern Caribbean

The largest Caribbean island nations are Cuba, the Dominican Republic and Haiti, followed by the Bahamas and Jamaica. Puerto Rico is a US Commonwealth, while the Cayman Islands and the Turks and Caicos Islands are British overseas territories. Most people are descended from Europeans, and Africans who came to the Caribbean as slaves. Sugar and coffee are leading crops. Manufacturing, mining and tourism are also important.

Fidel Castro led revolutionary forces to power in Cuba in 1959. His Communist policies and his close ties with the Soviet Union, which was dissolved in 1991, were opposed by the United States.

BAHAMAS

Area: 5,380sq miles (13,935sq km)
Population: 304,000
Capital: Nassau (pop 222,000)
Currency: Bahamian dollar

CUBA

Area: 42,804sq miles (110,861sq km)
Population: 11,383,000
Capital: Havana (pop 2,189,000)
Currency: Cuban peso

DOMINICAN REPUBLIC

Area: 18,816sq miles (48,734sq km)
Population: 9,184,000
Capital: Santo Domingo (pop 1,865,000)
Currency: Dominican peso

HAITI

Area: 10,714sq miles (27,750sq km)
Population: 8,309,000
Capital: Port-au-Prince (pop 1,961,000)
Currency: Gourde

JAMAICA

Area: 4,244sq miles (10,991sq km)
Population: 2,758,000
Capital: Kingston (pop 575,000)
Currency: Jamaican dollar

OVERSEAS TERRITORIES

CAYMAN ISLANDS (UK)
Area: 100sq miles (259sq km)
Population: 45,000
Capital: George Town

PUERTO RICO (US)
Area: 3,435sq miles (8,897sq km)
Population: 3,927,000
Capital: San Juan

TURKS AND CAICOS ISLANDS (UK)
Area: 166sq miles (430sq km)
Population: 21,000
Capital: Cockburn Town

Cricket is a major sport in Jamaica. It was introduced by the British, who ruled the island for about 300 years until it became independent in 1962. The official language in Jamaica is English.

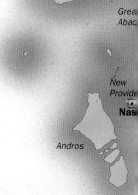
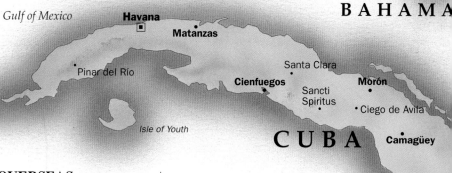

Little Abaco
Grand Bahama
Grea Abac
New Provide
Nas
Andros
Gulf of Mexico
Havana
Matanzas
BAHAMA
Pinar del Río
Santa Clara
Cienfuegos
Morón
Sancti Spiritus
• Ciego de Avila
Isle of Youth
CUBA
Camagüey
B

George Town

CAYMAN ISLANDS (UK)

Montego Bay
Spanish T
JAMAIC
Caribbean Se

Sugar cane is grown in many Caribbean islands and it is Cuba's leading export. The islands also produce minerals, including nickel (Cuba), iron and nickel (Dominican Republic) and bauxite (Jamaica).

Banking and other financial services are important in the Bahamas. Many foreign firms and banks have branches there. The islands have no direct taxes, so many people invest money in the banks.

Tourism is a major activity in the Caribbean. Swimming and snorkelling in the sparkling, sunlit water around the islands in the Bahamas are popular sports. More than 1.5 million tourists visit the Bahamas every year.

San Juan is the capital and largest city of Puerto Rico, a self-governing commonwealth in association with the United States. The chief jobs of the people are in manufacturing, trade and government.

Eleuthera

Cat

San Salvador

Rum Cay

Long

Crooked

Mayaguana

Acklins

Great Inagua

Great Exuma

Holguín

Guantánamo

Santiago de Cuba

·Cockburn Town

TURKS AND CAICOS ISLANDS (UK)

ATLANTIC OCEAN

Cap-Haïtien

Santiago

San Francisco

Gonaïves·

HAITI

DOMINICAN REPUBLIC

Port-au-Prince

La Romana

PUERTO RICO (US)

San Juan

Santo Domingo

Les Cayes

Jacmel

Ponce

0   100 miles

0   100 kilometers

Roman Catholicism was introduced into Cuba and the Dominican Republic by Spain, and into Haiti by France. But Protestantism is important in Jamaica and the Bahamas, which were influenced by Britain.

EASTERN CARIBBEAN

The eastern Caribbean consists mostly of small islands. Some are volcanic, while others are made of coral and limestone. The region contains eight independent countries and eight territories linked to France, the Netherlands, the United States and the UK. Farming and tourism are the chief activities, though Trinidad and Tobago has oil and natural gas. Native Americans once lived on the islands, but people of African descent now form the majority.

Road To

Charlotte Amalie
VIRGIN ISLAN

(US)

Dolphins of several species live in the waters of the Caribbean Sea. Tourists on cruise ships enjoy watching the dolphins. Fishing is an important industry, but nearly all of the catch is sold in local markets.

Tourism is a major industry in the eastern Caribbean. The islands are scenically beautiful and have many attractive, sun-baked beaches. Many people visit the islands on cruise ships.

Coconut

Sugar cane

Mace

Cloves

Nutmeg

Cinnamon

Spices, such as cinnamon and nutmeg, are grown on some of the islands in the eastern Caribbean. The main products of the islands include bananas, coconuts, cotton and sugar.

Massive eruptions of the Soufrière Hills volcano, on Montserrat, forced many people to leave their homes or leave the island in the late 1990s. The capital Plymouth was covered by volcanic ash and is now deserted.

ARUBA (Neth)   **NETHERLANDS ANTILLES**

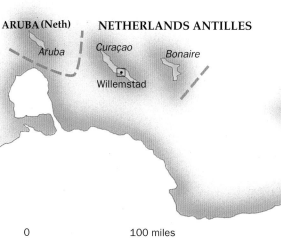

Aruba

Curaçao

Bonaire

Willemstad

0   100 miles

0   100 kilometers

S O U T H   A M E R I C A

Sailing and fishing are popular tourist activities in the blue waters of the Eastern Caribbean. Local people enjoy a variety of sports, including basketball, cricket and soccer.

ATLANTIC OCEAN

ANGUILLA (UK)
The Valley

ANTIGUA AND BARBUDA
Saint John's

Basseterre

ST KITTS AND NEVIS

Plymouth

MONTSERRAT (UK)

GUADELOUPE (Fr)
Basse Terre

DOMINICA
Roseau

Fort-de-France
MARTINIQUE (Fr)

Caribbean Sea

Castries
ST LUCIA

ST VINCENT AND THE GRENADINES
Kingstown

GRENADA
St George's

Tobago

TRINIDAD AND TOBAGO
Port of Spain
Trinidad

OVERSEAS TERRITORIES

ANGUILLA (UK)
Area: 37sq miles (96sq km)
Population: 13,000
Capital: The Valley

ARUBA (NETHERLANDS)
Area: 29sq miles (75sq km)
Population: 72,000
Capital: Oranjestad

GUADELOUPE (FRANCE)
Area: 658sq miles (1,705sq km)
Population: 453,000
Capital: Basse Terre

MARTINIQUE (FRANCE)
Area: 425sq miles (1,102sq km)
Population: 436,000
Capital: Fort-de-France

Bridgetown

BARBADOS

MONTSERRAT (UK)
Area: 39sq miles (102sq km)
Population: 9,000
Capital: Plymouth/Brades

NETHERLANDS ANTILLES
Area: 309sq miles (800sq km)
Population: 222,000
Capital: Willemstad

VIRGIN ISLANDS (US)
Area: 131sq miles (340sq km)
Population: 109,000
Capital: Charlotte Amalie

VIRGIN ISLANDS (UK)
Area: 59sq miles (153sq km)
Population: 23,000
Capital: Road Town

ANTIGUA AND BARBUDA

Area: 170sq miles (440sq km)
Population: 69,000
Capital: Saint John's (pop 28,000)
Currency: East Caribbean dollar

BARBADOS

Area: 166sq miles (431sq km)
Population: 280,000
Capital: Bridgetown (pop 80,000)
Currency: Barbados dollar

DOMINICA

Area: 290sq miles (751sq km)
Population: 69,000
Capital: Roseau (pop 27,000)
Currency: East Caribbean dollar

GRENADA

Area: 133sq miles (344sq km)
Population: 90,000
Capital: St George's (pop 33,000)
Currency: East Caribbean dollar

ST KITTS AND NEVIS

Area: 101sq miles (261sq km)
Population: 39,000
Capital: Basseterre (pop 13,000)
Currency: East Caribbean dollar

ST LUCIA

Area: 238sq miles (616sq km)
Population: 168,000
Capital: Castries (pop 67,000)
Currency: East Caribbean dollar

ST VINCENT AND THE GRENADINES

Area: 150sq miles (388sq km)
Population: 118,000
Capital: Kingstown (pop 29,000)
Currency: East Caribbean dollar

TRINIDAD AND TOBAGO

Area: 1,981sq miles (5,130sq km)
Population: 1,066,000
Capital: Port of Spain (pop 55,000)
Currency: Trinidad & Tobago dollar

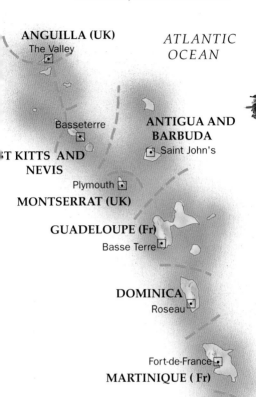

PEOPLE AND BELIEFS

North America contains eight percent of the world's population. Vast areas, including most of Canada and Alaska and the deserts of the southwestern United States and northern Mexico, are almost empty of people. Thickly populated areas, with many huge cities, occur in the eastern United States, California, the Mexican plateau, Central America and the Caribbean.

**Population densities
in North America**

Number of people
per square kilometer*

- Over 100
- Between 50 and 100
- Between 10 and 50
- Between 1 and 10
- Below 1

The main cities

- ■ Cities of more than
  1,000,000 people

- ● Cities of more than
  500,000 people

* 1 square kilometer = .4 square mile

Population and area

Although Canada is the world's second largest country, its population of over 30 million is only about one-ninth that of the United States and one-third that of Mexico. Around 200 years ago, more than 90 percent of North Americans lived in rural areas and farmed the land. Today 65 percent live in towns and cities, including Mexico City, the continent's largest, New York City, Los Angeles and Chicago.

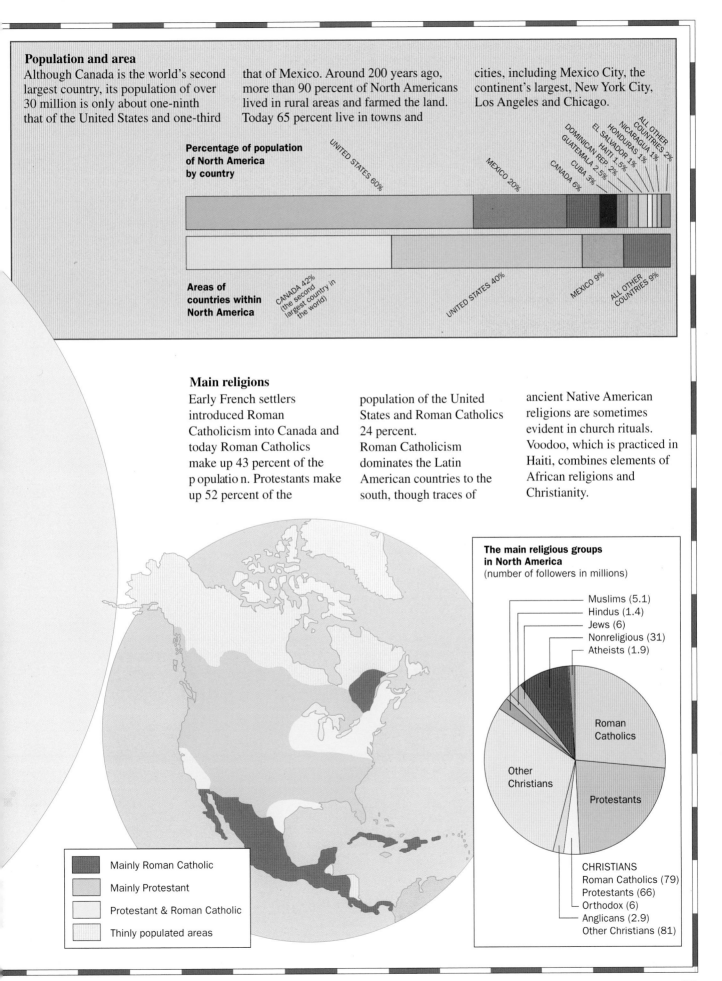

Percentage of population of North America by country

UNITED STATES 60%
MEXICO 20%
CANADA 6%
CUBA 3%
GUATEMALA 2.5%
DOMINICAN REP. 2%
HAITI 1.5%
EL SALVADOR 1.5%
HONDURAS 1%
NICARAGUA 1%
ALL OTHER COUNTRIES 2%

Areas of countries within North America

CANADA 42% (the second largest country in the world)
UNITED STATES 40%
MEXICO 9%
ALL OTHER COUNTRIES 9%

Main religions

Early French settlers introduced Roman Catholicism into Canada and today Roman Catholics make up 43 percent of the population. Protestants make up 52 percent of the population of the United States and Roman Catholics 24 percent. Roman Catholicism dominates the Latin American countries to the south, though traces of ancient Native American religions are sometimes evident in church rituals. Voodoo, which is practiced in Haiti, combines elements of African religions and Christianity.

Mainly Roman Catholic

Mainly Protestant

Protestant & Roman Catholic

Thinly populated areas

The main religious groups in North America
(number of followers in millions)

Muslims (5.1)
Hindus (1.4)
Jews (6)
Nonreligious (31)
Atheists (1.9)

Roman Catholics

Other Christians

Protestants

CHRISTIANS
Roman Catholics (79)
Protestants (66)
Orthodox (6)
Anglicans (2.9)
Other Christians (81)

CLIMATE AND VEGETATION

North America has every kind of climatic and vegetation region. The north is cold, but the United States has large areas of temperate forest and grasslands. Deserts cover parts of the southwestern United States, while southern Mexico, the Caribbean and Central America lie in the hot tropics.

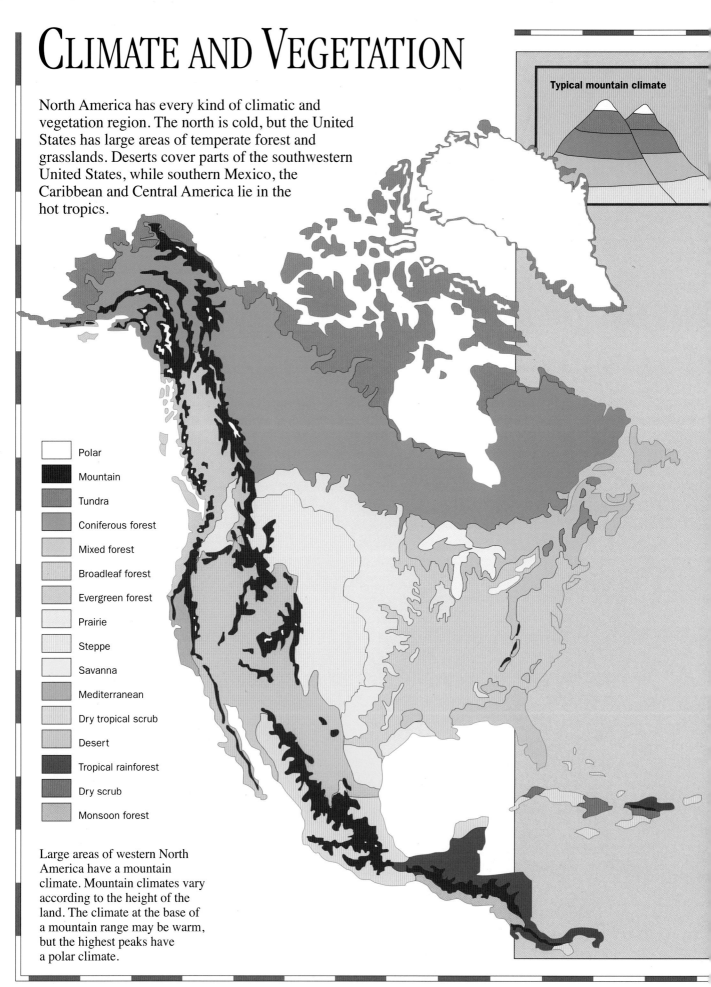

Typical mountain climate

Polar

Mountain

Tundra

Coniferous forest

Mixed forest

Broadleaf forest

Evergreen forest

Prairie

Steppe

Savanna

Mediterranean

Dry tropical scrub

Desert

Tropical rainforest

Dry scrub

Monsoon forest

Large areas of western North America have a mountain climate. Mountain climates vary according to the height of the land. The climate at the base of a mountain range may be warm, but the highest peaks have a polar climate.

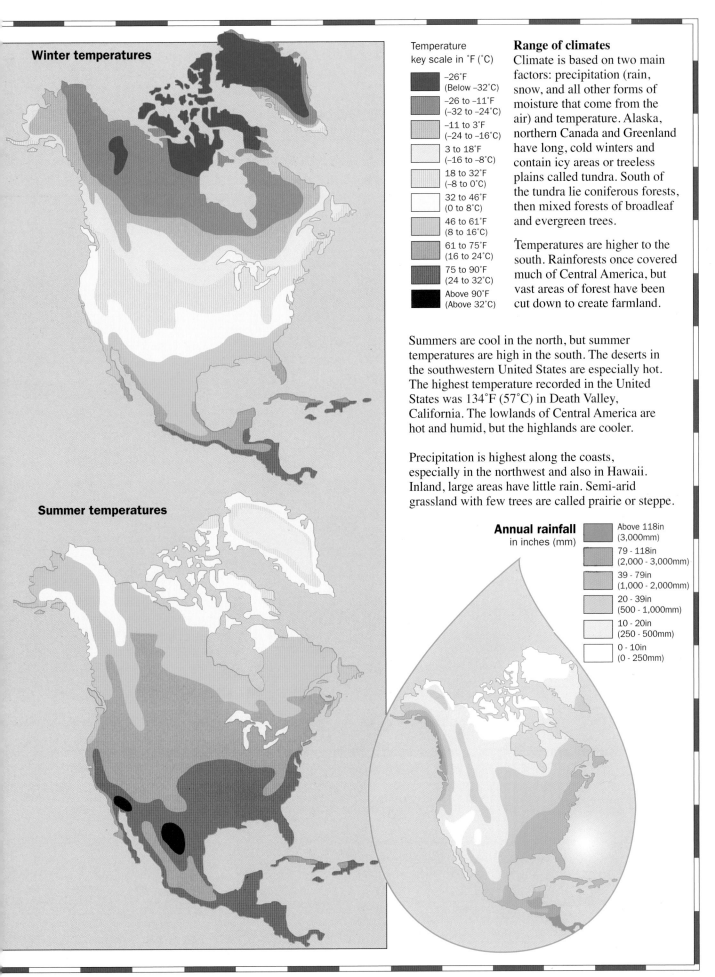

Winter temperatures

Summer temperatures

Temperature
key scale in °F (°C)

- –26°F (Below –32°C)
- –26 to –11°F (–32 to –24°C)
- –11 to 3°F (–24 to –16°C)
- 3 to 18°F (–16 to –8°C)
- 18 to 32°F (–8 to 0°C)
- 32 to 46°F (0 to 8°C)
- 46 to 61°F (8 to 16°C)
- 61 to 75°F (16 to 24°C)
- 75 to 90°F (24 to 32°C)
- Above 90°F (Above 32°C)

Range of climates

Climate is based on two main factors: precipitation (rain, snow, and all other forms of moisture that come from the air) and temperature. Alaska, northern Canada and Greenland have long, cold winters and contain icy areas or treeless plains called tundra. South of the tundra lie coniferous forests, then mixed forests of broadleaf and evergreen trees.

Temperatures are higher to the south. Rainforests once covered much of Central America, but vast areas of forest have been cut down to create farmland.

Summers are cool in the north, but summer temperatures are high in the south. The deserts in the southwestern United States are especially hot. The highest temperature recorded in the United States was 134°F (57°C) in Death Valley, California. The lowlands of Central America are hot and humid, but the highlands are cooler.

Precipitation is highest along the coasts, especially in the northwest and also in Hawaii. Inland, large areas have little rain. Semi-arid grassland with few trees are called prairie or steppe.

Annual rainfall
in inches (mm)

- Above 118in (3,000mm)
- 79 - 118in (2,000 - 3,000mm)
- 39 - 79in (1,000 - 2,000mm)
- 20 - 39in (500 - 1,000mm)
- 10 - 20in (250 - 500mm)
- 0 - 10in (0 - 250mm)

ECOLOGY AND ENVIRONMENT

The land is always changing. Natural forces, such as volcanic eruptions, great storms and unceasing erosion contribute to the change. People also change the land. Human activities cause pollution, while intensive farming exposes the land to the wind and rain, turning former grasslands into desert.

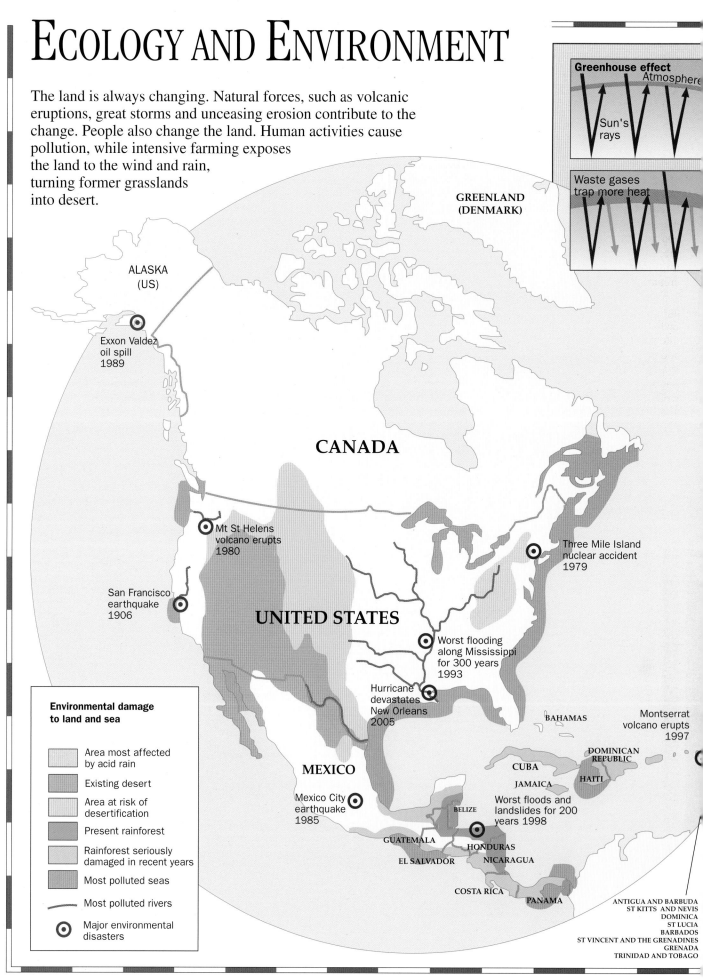

Greenhouse effect
Atmosphere
Sun's rays

Waste gases trap more heat

GREENLAND
(DENMARK)

ALASKA
(US)

Exxon Valdez
oil spill
1989

CANADA

Mt St Helens
volcano erupts
1980

Three Mile Island
nuclear accident
1979

San Francisco
earthquake
1906

UNITED STATES

Worst flooding
along Mississippi
for 300 years
1993

Hurricane
devastates
New Orleans
2005

BAHAMAS

Montserrat
volcano erupts
1997

DOMINICAN
REPUBLIC

MEXICO

CUBA

HAITI

JAMAICA

Mexico City
earthquake
1985

Worst floods and
landslides for 200
years 1998

BELIZE

GUATEMALA

HONDURAS

EL SALVADOR

NICARAGUA

COSTA RICA

PANAMA

ANTIGUA AND BARBUDA
ST KITTS AND NEVIS
DOMINICA
ST LUCIA
BARBADOS
ST VINCENT AND THE GRENADINES
GRENADA
TRINIDAD AND TOBAGO

**Environmental damage
to land and sea**

Area most affected
by acid rain

Existing desert

Area at risk of
desertification

Present rainforest

Rainforest seriously
damaged in recent years

Most polluted seas

Most polluted rivers

Major environmental
disasters

Damaging the environment

Air pollution is a problem in North America where factories, cars and homes emit waste gases into the air. Some gases dissolve in water vapor and cause acid rain, which kills trees. Excess carbon dioxide increases the atmosphere's natural greenhouse effect and may be causing global warming.

The clearing of forests and of grasslands lays soil bare. Strong winds and rain remove the topsoil making the land barren. The destruction of rainforests also threatens many living creatures with extinction.

Water pollution is caused by agricultural chemicals and waste from factories being washed or pumped into rivers and lakes, and by oil spills and untreated sewage at sea. Pollution is also caused by accidents at nuclear power stations. Today, people are working to combat pollution and its deadly effects.

Natural hazards

Earthquakes are common in western North America and the Caribbean, which lie on unstable parts of the earth's crust. Volcanic eruptions occur in Alaska, Washington, Mexico, Central America and the Caribbean. Hurricanes cause great damage in the Caribbean and the southeastern United States, while violent tornadoes tear through the central plains of the United States. Devastating floods occur when rivers overflow.

Natural hazards

 Earthquake zones

 Active volcanoes

 Hurricane tracks (June to October)

 Tornado danger areas

Endangered species

North America was once a vast, mostly empty wilderness, where many wild animals flourished. But in the last 400 years, hunting and the destruction of natural vegetation have greatly reduced the numbers of animals. Some species are close to extinction.

Fortunately, many endangered species are now protected and some have begun to recover their numbers. Even the bald eagle, symbol of the United States, was threatened, but the US government announced in 2007 that its numbers had recovered sufficiently for it to be removed from the endangered list after 40 years. The ivory-billed woodpecker, thought to be extinct, was rediscovered in 2004.

California condor

Some endangered species of North America

Birds
California condor
Eskimo curlew
Ivory-billed woodpecker

Mammals
Black bear
Black-footed ferret
Central American tapir
Jaguarundi
Polar bear
Volcano rabbit

Marine animals
Grey whale
Leatherback turtle
Manatee

Trees
Caribbean mahogany
Giant sequoia

41

ECONOMY

North America is rich in natural resources, including coal, oil, gas and most of the metals used in industry. It also has forests and large areas of fertile farmland. The most developed countries are the United States and Canada. Together, they produce about one-third of the world's industrial goods.

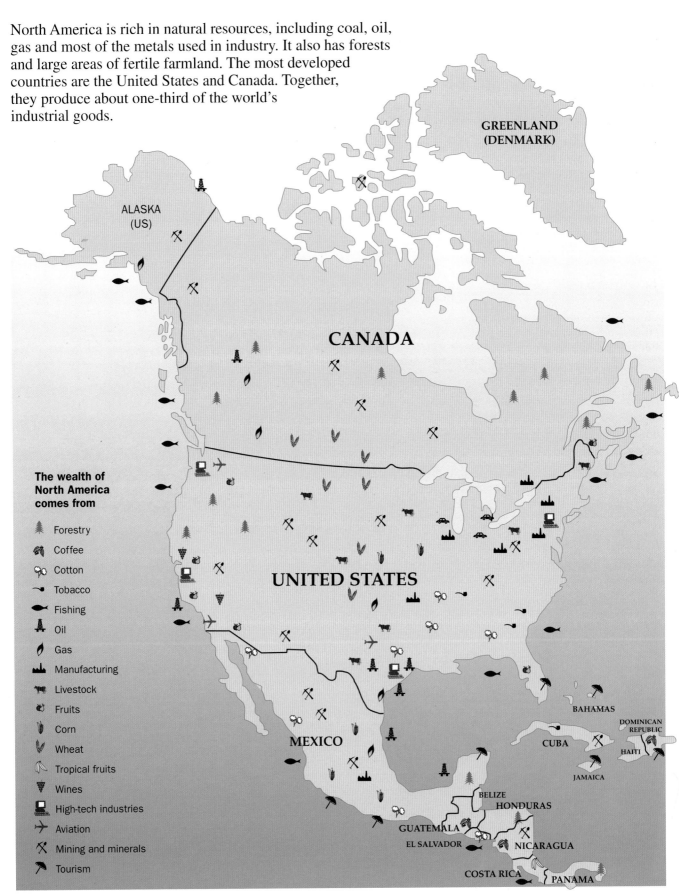

GREENLAND (DENMARK)

ALASKA (US)

CANADA

UNITED STATES

The wealth of North America comes from

- Forestry
- Coffee
- Cotton
- Tobacco
- Fishing
- Oil
- Gas
- Manufacturing
- Livestock
- Fruits
- Corn
- Wheat
- Tropical fruits
- Wines
- High-tech industries
- Aviation
- Mining and minerals
- Tourism

MEXICO

BAHAMAS

CUBA

DOMINICAN REPUBLIC

HAITI

JAMAICA

BELIZE

HONDURAS

GUATEMALA

EL SALVADOR

NICARAGUA

COSTA RICA

PANAMA

Gross domestic product

In order to compare the economies of countries, experts work out the gross domestic product (GDP) of the countries in US dollars. The GDP is the total value of all the goods and services produced in a country in a year. The chart, right, shows that the GDP of the United States is more than seven times bigger than the combined GDP of all the other countries in North America. No country in the world has a higher GDP than the United States.

GDP for the countries of North America
(in billions of dollars)

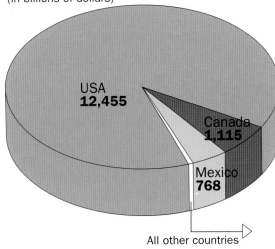

USA **12,455**

Canada **1,115**

Mexico **768**

All other countries

Cuba **40**
Guatemala **35**
Dominican Republic **28**
Costa Rica **19**
El Salvador **17**
Panama **15**
Trinidad and Tobago **15**
Jamaica **10**
Honduras **8**
Bahamas **6**
Nicaragua **5**
Haiti **4**
Barbados **3**
Belize **1**
Antigua and Barbuda **0.9**
St Lucia **0.8**
Grenada **0.5**
St Kitts and Nevis **0.5**
St Vincent and Grenadines **0.5**
Dominica **0.3**

Sources of energy

North America produces about a fifth of the world's oil. The leading producer is the United States, followed by Mexico, Canada, and Trinidad and Tobago. North America also produces about a third of the world's natural gas. Hydroelectricity (water power) is important, especially in Canada, while other important energy sources are coal and uranium.

In the United States, fossil fuels (coal, natural gas and oil) provide about three-quarters of the total energy produced. The burning of these fuels contributes to global warming. Nuclear energy and hydroelectricity are also important. Renewable sources are increasing.

Per capita GDPs

Per capita means per head or per person. Per capita GDPs are worked out by dividing the GDP by the population. For example, the per capita GDP of the United States is $41,700. Canada has a per capita GDP of $33,700. Haiti has a per capita GDP of only $510.

Sources of energy found in North America

🗄 Oil

🌢 Gas

≋ Hydroelectricity

⚒ Coal

☢ Uranium

ANTIGUA AND BARBUDA
ST KITTS AND NEVIS
DOMINICA
ST LUCIA
BARBADOS
ST VINCENT AND THE GRENADINES
GRENADA
TRINIDAD AND TOBAGO

POLITICS AND HISTORY

North America contains 23 independent countries. The United States and Mexico are federal republics. Canada, Belize and eight Caribbean nations are constitutional monarchies. They have their own governments, but they recognize the British monarch as their head of state. Ten countries are democratic republics, while Cuba is a Communist republic. North America also includes 14 overseas territories linked to Britain, Denmark, France, Netherlands and the United States.

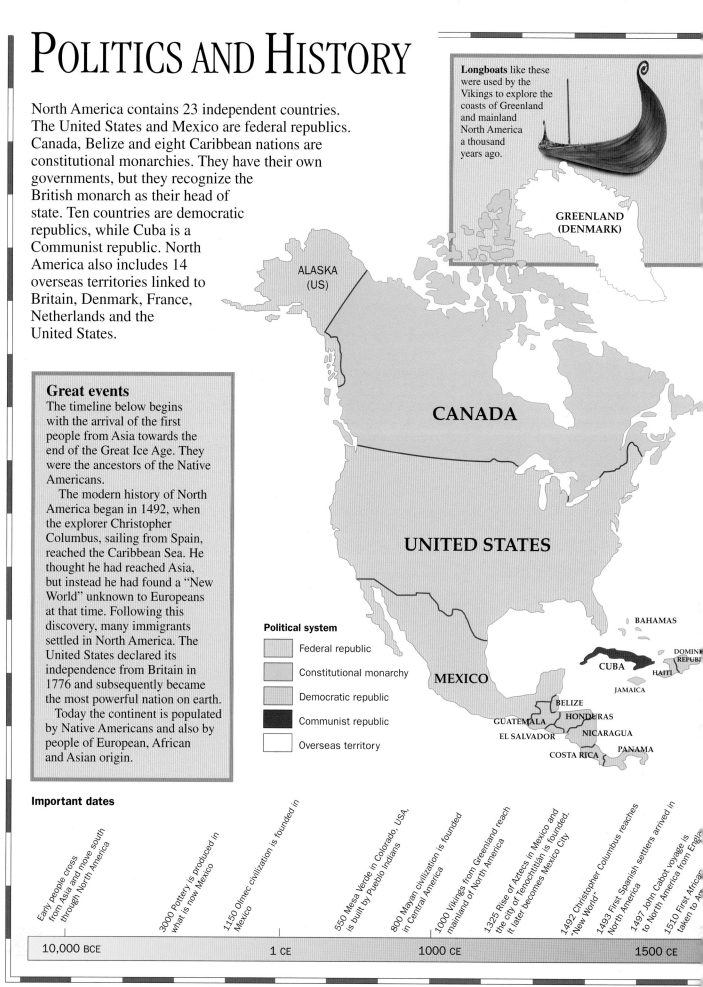

Longboats like these were used by the Vikings to explore the coasts of Greenland and mainland North America a thousand years ago.

GREENLAND (DENMARK)

ALASKA (US)

CANADA

UNITED STATES

MEXICO

BAHAMAS

CUBA

DOMINI REPUBI

HAITI

JAMAICA

BELIZE

GUATEMALA

HONDURAS

EL SALVADOR

NICARAGUA

COSTA RICA

PANAMA

Great events

The timeline below begins with the arrival of the first people from Asia towards the end of the Great Ice Age. They were the ancestors of the Native Americans.

The modern history of North America began in 1492, when the explorer Christopher Columbus, sailing from Spain, reached the Caribbean Sea. He thought he had reached Asia, but instead he had found a "New World" unknown to Europeans at that time. Following this discovery, many immigrants settled in North America. The United States declared its independence from Britain in 1776 and subsequently became the most powerful nation on earth.

Today the continent is populated by Native Americans and also by people of European, African and Asian origin.

Political system

- Federal republic
- Constitutional monarchy
- Democratic republic
- Communist republic
- Overseas territory

Important dates

Early people cross from Asia and move south through North America

3000 Pottery is produced in what is now Mexico

1150 Olmec civilization is founded in Mexico

550 Mesa Verde in Colorado, USA, is built by Pueblo Indians

800 Mayan civilization is founded in Central America

1000 Vikings from Greenland reach mainland of North America

1325 Rise of Aztecs in Mexico and the city of Tenochtitlán is founded. It later becomes Mexico City

1492 Christopher Columbus reaches "New World"

1493 First Spanish settlers arrived in North America

1497 John Cabot voyage is to North America from Engla

1510 First Africa taken to Ar

| 10,000 BCE | 1 CE | 1000 CE | 1500 CE |

44

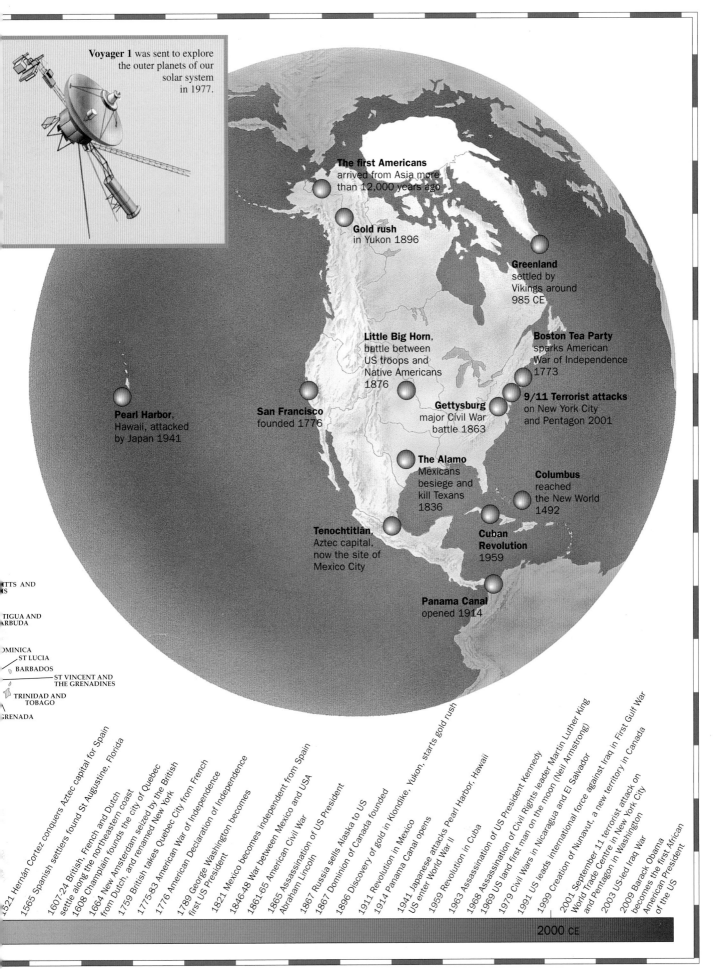

Voyager 1 was sent to explore the outer planets of our solar system in 1977.

The first Americans arrived from Asia more than 12,000 years ago

Gold rush in Yukon 1896

Greenland settled by Vikings around 985 CE

Little Big Horn, battle between US troops and Native Americans 1876

Boston Tea Party sparks American War of Independence 1773

9/11 Terrorist attacks on New York City and Pentagon 2001

San Francisco founded 1776

Gettysburg major Civil War battle 1863

Pearl Harbor, Hawaii, attacked by Japan 1941

The Alamo Mexicans besiege and kill Texans 1836

Columbus reached the New World 1492

Tenochtitlán, Aztec capital, now the site of Mexico City

Cuban Revolution 1959

Panama Canal opened 1914

TTS AND
S

TIGUA AND
RBUDA

OMINICA
ST LUCIA

BARBADOS

ST VINCENT AND
THE GRENADINES

TRINIDAD AND
TOBAGO

GRENADA

1521 Hernán Cortez conquers Aztec capital for Spain

1565 Spanish settlers found St Augustine, Florida

1607-24 British, French and Dutch settle along the northeastern coast

1608 Champlain founds the city of Québec

1664 New Amsterdam seized by the British from Dutch, and renamed New York

1759 British takes Quebec City from French

1775-83 American War of Independence

1776 American Declaration of Independence

1789 George Washington becomes first US President

1821 Mexico becomes independent from Spain

1846-48 War between Mexico and USA

1861-65 American Civil War

1865 Assassination of US President Abraham Lincoln

1867 Russia sells Alaska to US

1867 Dominion of Canada becomes

1896 Discovery of gold in Klondike, Yukon, starts gold rush

1911 Revolution in Mexico

1914 Panama Canal opens

1941 Japanese attacks Pearl Harbor, Hawaii US enter World War II

1959 Revolution in Cuba

1963 Assassination of US President Kennedy

1968 Assassination of Civil Rights leader Martin Luther King

1969 US land first man on the moon (Neil Armstrong)

1979 Civil Wars in Nicaragua and El Salvador

1991 US leads international force against Iraq in First Gulf War

1999 Creation of Nunavut, a new territory in Canada

2001 September 11 terrorist attack on World Trade Centre in New York City and Pentagon in Washington

2003 US-led Iraq War

2009 Barack Obama becomes the first African American President of the US

2000 CE

GLOSSARY

assassinate To murder by surprise attack.

barren Not producing crops or fruit.

besiege To close in on; to surround; to hem in with armed forces for a prolonged attack.

colony A territory distant from the state that has control over it.

commonwealth A federation of states.

coniferous Cone-bearing trees.

conserve To save; to keep from being lost, damaged, or wasted.

constitutional monarchy A form of government in which a king or queen is a figurehead leader, while actual political and legislative power rests with executive, legislative, and judicial branches of the government.

empire A group of states or territories under the control of a single ruling person, family, or corporation.

export To send to another country for the purposes of sale.

extinction Destroying or being destroyed.

fertile Producing abundantly; rich in resources; fruitful.

forerunner A predecessor or ancestor.

gumbo A soup thickened with unripe okra pods.

tributary A stream that flows into a larger stream or river.

income Money or other gain received by an individual or corporation.

majestic Very grand or dignified.

manufacture The making of goods by hand or by machine.

microprocessor The controlling unit of a computer, laid out on a tiny silicon chip and responsible for handling data, performing calculations, and carrying out stored instructions.

migrate To move from one region to another with the change of seasons.

nucleus A thing or part forming the center around which other things or parts are grouped or collected; a core.

pastime A way of spending spare time pleasantly.

pelt The skin of a fur-bearing animal.

petroleum Oily, flammable liquid that, when distilled, makes paraffin, fuel oil, kerosene, and gasoline.

pharmacist A person licensed to prepare and dispense drugs.

plumage A bird's feathers.

precipitation A falling of rain, snow, or sleet.

predator A creature that hunts, kills, and feeds on other creatures.

probe A spacecraft designed to explore the upper atmosphere, space, or a celestial body, like a planet or moon.

remote Far off; far away.

republic A system of government in which the power rests with citizens who are entitled to vote and is exercised by popularly-elected representatives.

rural Living in the country; having to do with farming.

spectacle An unusual sight; something strange or remarkable to look at.

FOR MORE INFORMATION

American Museum of Natural History
Central Park West at 79th Street
New York, NY 10024-5192
(212) 769-5606
Web site: http://www.amnh.org/home/?src=toolbar
The museum's mission is to discover, interpret, and disseminate—through scientific research and education—knowledge about human cultures, the natural world, and the universe.

Canadian Museum of Civilization
100 Laurier Street
Gatineau, PQ, Canada K1A 0M8
Web site: http://www.civilization.ca/cmc/home/cmc-home
Canada's largest and most popular cultural institution.

Greenland National Museum & Archives
Hans Egedevej 8
P.O.Box 145
3900 Nuuk
Phone: (+299) 32 26 11
The Greenland National Museum and Archives preserves Greenland's cultural heritage. The museum is the central institution for research and documentation of cultural history and is also the central archival institution for public archives and offices.

National Museum of the American Indian
The George Gustav Heye Center
Alexander Hamilton US Custom House
One Bowling Green
New York, NY 10004
(212) 514-3700
Web site: http://www.nmai.si.edu/index.cfm
The National Museum of the American Indian is the first national museum dedicated to the preservation, study, and exhibition of the life, languages, literature, history, and arts of Native Americans. Established by an act of Congress in 1989, the museum works in collaboration with the Native peoples of the Western Hemisphere to protect and foster their cultures by reaffirming traditions and beliefs, encouraging contemporary artistic expression, and empowering the Indian voice.

National Museum of Anthropology
Reforma and Gandhi
Chapultepec Polanco
Mexico City, Mexico, D.F.
Phone: (52) 5553-6381
This museum shows Mexico's native history, from the remote past to the present time. Includes archeological objects and artifacts associated with the ethnic groups that inhabit Mexico.

Smithsonian National Museum of American History
14th Street and Constitution Avenue, NW
Washington, DC 20560
(202) 357-2700
Web site: http://americanhistory.si.edu/index.cfm
The Smithsonian's National Museum of American History dedicates its collections and scholarship to inspiring a broader understanding of the United States and its many peoples. The Museum collects and preserves more than 3 million artifacts—all true national treasures. Its collections form a fascinating mosaic of American life and comprise the greatest single collection of American history.

WEB SITES

Due to the changing nature of Internet links, Rosen Publishing has developed an online list of Web sites related to the subject of this book. This site is updated regularly. Please use this link to access the list:

http://www.rosenlinks.com/atl/namer

FOR FURTHER READING

Adovasio, J. M., and Jake Page. *The First Americans: In Pursuit of Archaeology's Greatest Mystery*. New York, NY: Modern Library, 2003.

Bockenhauer, Mark H. *Our Fifty States*. Des Moines, IA: National Geographic Children's Books, 2004.

Daniels, Patricia S., and Steve Hyslop. *National Geographic Almanac of World History*. Des Moines, IA: National Geographic, 2006.

de Blij, H. J. *Atlas of North America*. New York, NY: Oxford University Press, 2005.

Fagan, Brian M. *Ancient North America*. New York, NY: Thames & Hudson, 2005.

Hardwick, Susan W., et al. *The Geography of North America: Environment, Political Economy, and Culture*. Upper Saddle River, NJ: Prentice Hall, 2007.

Johnson, Michael, and Richard Hook. *Encyclopedia of Native Tribes of North America*. New York, NY: Firefly Books, 2007.

Kagan, Neil. *National Geographic Concise History of the World: An Illustrated Time Line*. Des Moines, IA: National Geographic, 2006.

Miller, James, and John Thompson. *National Geographic Almanac of American History*. Des Moines, IA: National Geographic, 2007.

National Geographic. *National Geographic Essential Visual History of the World*. Des Moines, IA: National Geographic, 2007.

Oxford University Press. *New Concise World Atlas*. New York, NY: Oxford University Press, 2007.

Rowell, Galen. *North America the Beautiful* (Journeys through the World). Vercelli, Italy: White Star, 2006.

Sutton, Mark Q. *An Introduction to Native North America*. Upper Saddle River, NJ: Allyn & Bacon, 2007.

INDEX

ABOUT THE AUTHORS

Tina Lundgren lives in Robbinsville, NJ.

Malcolm Porter is a leading children's cartographer. He has contributed to the *Times Atlas* and *Reader's Digest Atlas*. He has collaborated on geographical series and provided maps for leading educational and trade publishers including HarperCollins, BBC, Kingfisher, Rand McNally, and Doubleday. He drew the maps and designed Doubleday's award-winning *Atlas of the United States of America* and the *Collins Children's Atlas*. In collaboration with Keith Lye, he drew original maps, illustrations, and did the designs for all six books in Rosen Publishing's Atlases of the World series.

Keith Lye is a best-selling author of geography titles for children of all ages, including several atlases. He is a distinguished contributor and consultant to major encyclopedias including *Encyclopaedia Britannica and World Book*. Many of his titles have won awards.